D1707637

BAYOU D'ARBONNE SWAMP

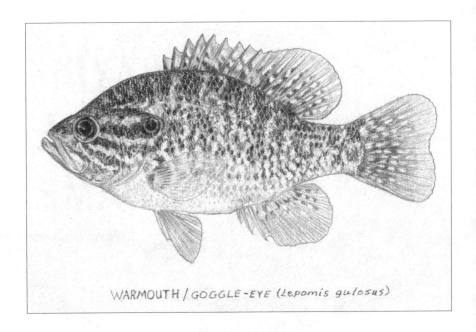

WARMOUTH / GOGGLE-EYE (Lepomis gulosus)

BAYOU D'ARBONNE SWAMP

A NATURALIST'S MEMOIR OF PLACE

Kelby Ouchley

Louisiana State University Press

Baton Rouge

Published by Louisiana State University Press
lsupress.org

Manufactured in the United States of America
FIRST PRINTING

DESIGNER: Mandy McDonald Scallan
TYPEFACE: Calluna
PRINTER AND BINDER: Versa Press, Inc.

Jacket photograph is reproduced courtesy of Jenny Ellerbe.

Library of Congress Cataloging-in-Publication Data
Names: Ouchley, Kelby, 1951– author.
Title: Bayou D'Arbonne swamp : a naturalist's memoir of place / Kelby
    Ouchley.
Description: Baton Rouge : Louisiana State University Press, [2022] |
    Includes bibliographical references.
Identifiers: LCCN 2021057418 (print) | LCCN 2021057419 (ebook) | ISBN
    978-0-8071-7731-0 (cloth) | ISBN 978-0-8071-7830-0 (pdf) | ISBN 978-0-8071-7829-4
    (epub)
Subjects: LCSH: Natural history—Louisiana—Bayou D'Arbonne Lake. |
    Bayous—Louisiana.
Classification: LCC QH105.L8 O925 2022 (print) | LCC QH105.L8 (ebook) |
    DDC 508.763/89—dc23/eng/20220317
LC record available at https://lccn.loc.gov/2021057418
LC ebook record available at https://lccn.loc.gov/2021057419

To my daughters-in-law,

Julie Kay Ouchley and

Winnie Nguyen Ouchley

PREFACE

In the beginning there was mud, bayou mud, molding my ontogeny just as it had formed the shell-tempered vessels of other residents since gone to earth. The summer of 1964 was the beginning for me, when I was thirteen and loosed upon the bayou and its swamp for the first time. Rules were minimal. Even the "be home by dark" decree was rescinded by autumn. An intimacy with local geology started with the half-mile, barefoot walk from home to the bayou. Home was on the hill at an elevation safe from backwater flooding. Hiking north and descending toward the bayou, I tramped old sandy-clay soils of the tertiary epoch that gave way to new dark silt-loams of the active floodplain. Alluvial mud comprised of this younger dirt and swamp water was adjacent to and under the bayou, wherever it happened to be in its seasonal wanderings. Extrasensory when encountered, mud became the pilings upon which I constructed my definition of this environment.

The odor of summer mud imprints first. It is pungent with a bit of putrid decay, the telltale exhaust of the solar-powered, biological engine that powers the D'Arbonne Swamp. In time the odor becomes alluring, even haunting. Eventually, it settles onto the first cranial nerve and becomes a memory aroma. From this point forward the odor overwhelmed the man I became with distinct images of adolescent experiences. They appear most vividly when I approach the water's edge after having been away from Louisiana bayous and rivers for a long time—seining a sandbar on a stormy night, checking trotlines at dawn with great anticipation.

As a visual stimulus when the bayou is at summertime lows, mud exists as gray riparian bands cracking along the upper edges. To a bank-fishing boy awash in the freedom of the natural world, this contrasting landscape is enthralling. At irregular intervals along the shoreline, colorful groups of young male butterflies huddle to sip minerals, often in urine-soaked tracks of white-tailed deer. The bright butterfly clusters flush at passing dragonflies and settle back to the mud like whirling confetti. Also scattered along the bank and reflecting sunlight in nacreous hues of blushed pink and cerulean are the shells of freshwater mussels. They are the remains of creatures with names such as threehorn wartyback, little spectaclecase, and Texas lilliput.

Clarity is not a trait of this or most bayous. If as a boy I waded out in the water up to my knees to salvage a goggle-eye-tangled fishing line, I would have been lucky to see the tops of my feet. Mud at this depth appears chocolate-colored but transforms into ever-brighter shades of olive closer to the shoreline. This film of algae can exist only in the narrow strip where sunlight penetrates the water column. At greater depths the photons of light cannot dodge all of the suspended clay particles and are thus absorbed or reflected. In the shallows, though, algae capture the sunbeams in an alchemist's plot and release oxygen so that the goggle-eye bream and his pursuer might breathe on a hot summer day.

After olfactory and visual characteristics of bayou mud are considered, only one of the five human senses remains to be discussed, as mud is silent and tastes as you would expect. For me, the tactile experiences of mud fill the bookshelves of my memory only second in volume to odors. Imagine the rough, sunbaked texture of cracked mud in mid-August. Fissures in gray geometric patterns irritate even the late-summer soles of bare feet. Imagine also on this day, when the humidity is close behind a temperature that approaches the century mark, a sensation of cold, silky velvet that envelops the lower extremities as deep as a boy can bury them by wading out and wiggling his toes mole-like toward the center of the earth. Words can't do bayou mud justice.

Place cannot be depicted on a map, which in most cases only represents space and the juxtaposition of physical features like rivers and mountains as defined by measureable units. This strictly geographic tact disregards unquantifiable elements of place that are intangible yet vital components:

history, memories, meaning, and essence. These are recognized and absorbed according to one's individual umwelt, experiences, and trails that have beckoned.

Accordingly, the paths within this book are not straight. They wander all over the place, and the place is Bayou D'Arbonne Swamp in north Louisiana. Like most places in North America, the swamp has deep geologic history and a shallow human history, especially for those of us not of Amerindian descent. Even thinner is the timeline of one writer's life in this place. A natural history also rests on the surface of the swamp, evolving with the biota in slow time. The paths run alongside these parts and over foot logs that span facts, speculations, stories, and connections. How does one write a place if not by walking its paths with a pen?

These then are the stories of a swamp. Although they are the stories of a particular swamp, they have relevance to other swamps, even prairies, mountains, and deserts if viewed through an ecological, social, or historical lens. Many are stories of how modern humans change natural areas, including their flora and fauna. They are also my stories as a boy and man, as a wildlife biologist, resource manager, and naturalist.

ACKNOWLEDGMENTS

A memoir is a story of one's life experiences. Most people's stories are filled with interactions with others, some of whom impact and enrich the personal narrative. In my case it was grandparents, parents, siblings, my spouse and two sons, and other relatives. My cast also included boyhood friends like David Acree, Johnny Lewis, Criswell White, and Mike Wilbanks, and sages like Lea Ouchley Franks, Nicky Haye, and Donnie Wainwright. Influential educators and professional colleagues are too numerous to mention but nevertheless important.

Biologists Gypsy Hanks and Mike Wood contributed valuable data for this project. Historian Tim Hudson's scholarly work in the area is unsurpassed and much appreciated. MaryLynn Dobson, Ann Bloxom Smith, and my wife, Amy, provided helpful comments on early drafts. William Caverlee conducted a very constructive edit. LSU Press Editor-in-Chief Rand Dotson and Managing Editor Catherine Kadair shepherded the publication process in a most professional manner.

I am indeed fortunate to have family members and friends who are artists, both professional and avocational. Several enthusiastically agreed to contribute their valuable time and talent in the form of illustrations and photographs created purposely for this book. They include Gay Brantley, Leigh Buffington, Emily Caldwell, Jenny Ellerbe, Gypsy Hanks, Amy Ouchley, Susan Ouchley, Zach Ouchley, and Anna Rowan. I can't thank them enough.

BAYOU D'ARBONNE SWAMP

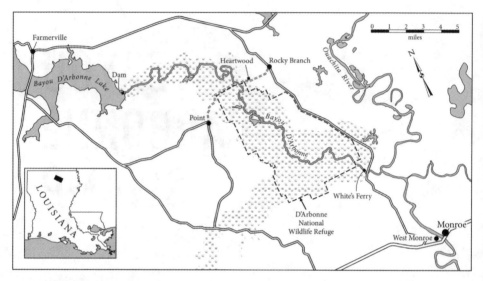

D'Arbonne Swamp. Map by Mary Lee Eggart.

1

Bayou D'Arbonne Swamp—Early Memories—Geography

"Bayou" is a word that perplexes those unfamiliar with the "Bayou State." The term is ubiquitous here, as a broad range of businesses advertise the word in their names. There is a Bayou Bowling Alley, Bayou Gymnastics, Bayou Internet, Bayou Plumbing, and many others. "Bayou" shows up in the names of churches and school mascots. Early Choctaw Indians would be mystified by all this hoopla since they were responsible for the etymology of the word. French settlers took the Native Americans' perfectly good word *bayuk* and contorted it into the Franco-label "bayou." The definition, however, remains the same. It is a natural, relatively small waterway that flows through swamps and other lowlands. More than four hundred named bayous braid Louisiana from north to south seeking the shortest route to the Gulf of Mexico across a landscape void of significant relief. A few creep into the flat fringes of Arkansas, Mississippi, and Texas. Except during flood events, currents in bayous are usually sluggish or absent. Crystalline waters are not a characteristic of bayous as they meander through heavy clay soils and capture the washed-in silt of subtropical rains. Their shores are often dressed in live oaks and big-butted cypress trees laden with Spanish moss and parula warblers. Inhabitants of bayous are not without their own notable reputations and include crawfish, cottonmouths, mosquito larvae, alligator gar, alligator snapping turtles, and alligators. Plenty of others, more innocuous in their life cycles, are dependent on these sinuous southern streams.

In this part of the world, the names that stuck on early maps and remain today are frequently of French origin because of early French-Canadian hunter/explorers from the north and later French administrators from the south. Most fall into one of two categories: ties to a French surname or else reference to a natural feature including biota. Bayou de l'Outre (otter bayou) is an example of the latter, and Bayou D'Arbonne represents the former. The derivation of the present name, Bayou D'Arbonne, is tied to the genealogy of one family, and a best guess points to Jean Baptiste d'Arbonne (1752–1829) as the namesake. Jean Baptiste was the son of Jean-Baptiste d'Arbonne of Natchitoches, and both were descendants of Gaspard Derbanne, a Canadian hunter who accompanied Louis Jucherneau St. Denis during his exploration of the Red River Valley in 1714. An early mention of the stream's current name is found in a report to Spanish Governor Galvez by Ouachita Post Commandant Jean-Baptist Filhiol in 1784. It should be noted that the d'Arbonne surname varies in the literature as Darban, Derbanne, Darbanne, Derban, and Darbonne. Whether anyone with any of these names actually gazed on the bayou's waters in the eighteenth century is unknown. Today, colloquial terminology for the bayou is "the D'Arbonne" (pronounced DAR-bone), and Bayou D'Arbonne Swamp is just referred to as "the swamp."

A swamp is a wetland that is dominated by woody plants. A critical characteristic is that the water table must recede often enough to a depth that allows root aeration and survival of adapted trees and shrubs. These are the traits of Bayou D'Arbonne Swamp.

I distinctly remember when I was four years old going with my father in his early 1950s cream-colored Ford down to the D'Arbonne at the mouth of Rocky Branch where he target-practiced with his Marlin .30-30 deer rifle. It is not a pleasant memory. Much to the disgust of my father, the explosions terrified me, and I ran to cover my ears, crouched on the hump of the back-seat floorboard. Today, ironically, I can no longer hear the high, sewing-machine trill of pine warblers after shooting firearms for six decades.

I recall, soon after the target-practice incident, sitting on an overturned lard bucket in a cypress john boat as my grandfather paddled down the D'Arbonne. He was by nature a quiet man of medium build with crow-wing black hair like my father, a trait that many said was evidence of their Native American heritage. I barely knew him as he succumbed to lung cancer when

I was ten years old. On this early summer morning we were on a fishing trip, but for the life of me I could not understand how we were going to catch fish without bait. When I had mentioned this problem earlier, Papaw Wilburn didn't seem to be worried. He paddled along leisurely until abruptly changing course to tie up to the overhanging limbs of a water elm. By then I was becoming anxious to fish, and when he reached down for the morning newspaper that was just too much for me. A patient "Hold on, boy" was less reprimand than I deserved as his plan played out. He wrapped several sheets of the newspaper around a cane pole and tied it on with an old shoestring. Then he struck a kitchen match by rubbing it along the side of his leather shoe and set the newspaper afire. Abruptly standing in the low-sided bateau, he raised the torch overhead and began poking a dinner-plate-sized red-wasp nest that I had until this point not been aware of. The idea was to kill the adult wasps with flames and use their larvae for fish bait. For a prescient five-year-old boy the incident was thought-provoking to say the least as I received an early lesson in swamp improvisation. I don't remember if we caught supper.

In a few more years I was let loose on the D'Arbonne and its swamp that beckoned from the bottom of the red clay hill where we lived. While camping in the heart of the swamp with neighborhood boys, I learned from Mr. Tink, a local sage in such matters, how to fish for giant alligator gar in the shallow pools by using a long, cottonwood pole with a short wire leader and huge 20/0 hooks baited with whole gaspergou. The floating pole was tossed in the bayou and would stand on end when the bait was struck. Eating the hot, deep-fried chunks of gar on the bayou bank at sunset branded memories on the sunburned hides of hungry boys. So did the calls of barred owls and the screams of panthers that always turned out to be great-uncle Clarence, who would hike barefooted through the swamp to our remote campsite and arrive just after we collapsed exhausted on army cots draped with mosquito bars. These early memories were the foundation for a sense of place infinitely more complex than I could imagine at the time.

Within the Bayou D'Arbonne watershed of 1.2 million acres, three medium-sized streams approach from the northwest and merge to form one large channel near the present town of Farmerville, Louisiana. Corney Bayou, and its tributaries with headwaters in Columbia and Union Counties, Arkansas, is the northernmost. It is dammed within the Corney Lake Unit of Kisatchie National Forest to form Corney Lake (2,300 acres). Middle Fork Creek runs parallel to Corney a few miles further south, and below it Bayou D'Arbonne proper, beginning in Claiborne Parish, flows through the red clay hills. The upper portion of this fork is dammed to form Lake Claiborne (6,400 acres). The confluence of the three streams is now drowned beneath Bayou D'Arbonne Lake (15,280 acres) in Union Parish. From the Bayou D'Arbonne Lake dam the consolidated bayou continues to flow southeast into Ouachita Parish where it empties into the Ouachita River just above Monroe.

Bayou D'Arbonne owns the remaining swamp below the dam, created it, nourishes it, shapes it yet. The swamp would vanish without the bayou. Beginning eleven thousand years ago, the fledgling stream started meandering through 50-million-year-old Eocene deposits left behind by a receding sea, scouring them away to depths up to a hundred feet. For more than ten millennia the bayou has whip-sawed across this arena creating new channels, abandoning old ones, leaving in its wake point bars, oxbows, natural levees, and meander scars. It pushed up a moderate terrace on the east side, and between this low ridge and the hills of old soil on the west began depositing alluvial sediments to create a floodplain for the swamp. The resulting topography is flat, varying by only twenty feet of elevation across the broad floodplain; relief is almost imperceptible to the untrained eye. A combination of level landscape and fifty inches of annual rainfall in a subtropical climate yields only one outcome—wetlands.

Wetlands are areas where the water table is at or near the surface for much of the growing season in most years, resulting in long periods of soil saturation and specialized vegetation adapted to wet conditions. That most of the volume of plants in Bayou D'Arbonne Swamp are trees and shrubs makes this wetland a swamp by definition. It is the extent of flooding, however, that makes it the wettest type of swamp—a deep overflow swamp. People unfamiliar with this area are astounded when I lead a summer hike into the powder-dry swamp and point out a line of crusty filamentous algae twenty feet up in an overcup oak as the water level two months earlier. Flooding to a depth of ten feet above the floodplain for several months each year is common, and extreme events of thirty-feet inundations are increasing occurrences. In recent times, hundred-year floods as defined by the US Army Corps of Engineers have misplaced their calendars. Picture in your mind, then, this swamp varying in width from one to five miles along both sides of Bayou D'Arbonne as it meanders twenty-seven miles from the dam to the Ouachita River. Encompassing twenty-four thousand acres of forested wetlands, it is easily delineated on a map. As a "place," though, it is more than boundaries.

2

The Original Inhabitants—Lessons from the First People

Humans arrived at this place during the gestation period of the swamp, about twelve thousand years ago at the end of the Late Pleistocene period. They encountered an environment much cooler than today and with greater fluctuations in seasonal temperatures. We would barely recognize the vegetation. Cold-loving spruce forests were being replaced with mixed hardwood forests of oak and hickory throughout, with southern pines emerging in the uplands. It was a mosaic of forest types and grasslands in the midst of great natural change, all in response to the retreating glaciers a thousand miles to the north. The people, known as Paleoindians, were hunter-gatherers and roamed across the landscape hunting now-extinct megafauna such as mastodons, giant sloths, and bison. No doubt they were opportunistic foragers of smaller game also, as well as of a multitude of native plants. Since their population levels were low, their surviving traces are sparse and nonexistent in the swamp proper because its surface is too young. Only in the old, adjacent hills on rare occasions do their diagnostic, fluted projectile points betray their ancient presence.

Time flowed into the Holocene, the current geological epoch, as the flora and fauna of the swamp and its environs came closer to resembling that of today. Within the Holocene, the term "Archaic" describes both the time period of 10,000 to 2,800 years ago and the lifestyle of the people for much of the era—still egalitarian hunting-and-gathering societies. By the Middle Archaic, evidence of a transformative new technology emerges in archaeological sites with the atlatl or spear thrower. The spears, which now had a greatly extended range for hunting wary animals like deer, were armed with lanceolate Dalton points and later by corner-notched San Patrice points. It is noteworthy that true arrowheads did not exist in the Archaic, as the bow and arrow was not invented here until thousands of years later. All stone projectile points of Archaic age armed darts or spears and occur only on the old surfaces around the swamp.

By the Middle Archaic people seemed to have become more sedentary with seasonal campsites along the bayous and rivers and more permanent settlements in the nearby hills. Large megafauna were now extinct and the focus shifted to abundant aquatic resources. Screening of materials from these sites has revealed remains of catfish, freshwater drum, buffalo (fish), gar, turtles, mussels, and aquatic snails. Traces of deer, small mammals, and wild plants including acorns and hickory nuts remained plentiful. Then, about 5,500 years ago and thirteen miles below the mouth of Bayou D'Arbonne, something happened that when discovered and interpreted would upend the field of North American archaeology and result in a 1997 cover story of *Science* magazine.

The sea-change in scholarly thought began when the Louisiana state archaeologist for this region, Dr. Joe Saunders, using radio-carbon dating, revealed that eleven mounds and other earthworks known as the Watson Brake site located on the Pleistocene terrace just west of the modern Ouachita River were occupied between 5,500 and 4,800 years ago. As the "most securely dated early mound site in North America," Watson Brake is two thousand years older than Poverty Point World Heritage Site, which rises up out of the Mississippi delta forty-five miles to the east and was once thought to be the most ancient mound system on the continent. As a reference point, Watson Brake is also much older than the Egyptian pyramids. Before Dr. Saunders proved otherwise, it was believed that people of this time period were not socially organized with work leaders and laborers necessary to build monumental earthworks. Such hierarchy with chiefs and peons could not occur until agriculture replaced hunting and gathering and thus could feed the large number of people required, and this would not happen for several thousand years. Or so it was thought. Of all the remarkable revelations of Watson Brake, the most telling is that the natural resources of the adjacent river and surrounding swamps and forests were indeed rich and plentiful enough to support a lot of people for a long time. Since the embryonic D'Arbonne Swamp was within easy foraging range of Watson Brake by paddle or foot, it surely contributed to their larder.

The Archaic period was followed by the Woodland period, which lasted from 2,800 to 800 years ago. The bow and arrow arrived locally between AD 300 and 600. Ceramics or pottery appeared early in the period, initially in the form of crude, sand-tempered pots followed by those incorporating the technological advances of grog- and then shell-tempering for durability. Archaeologists often define the various cultures within this period by the composition and decorations of their ceramics. Today, enigmatic sherds of vessels and true arrowheads that were shaped by unknown hands are sprinkled across every ridge in the swamp. As the quality of pottery improved throughout the Woodland period, the craftsmanship of stone artifacts such as points and knives mysteriously declined. Artifacts were no longer made from finely worked flints that originated far to the north or east and arrived here via trade networks. Woodland-period artifacts were formed from local cherts less suitable for knapping. Just as the bayou continued to change its channel on the floodplain, so too did the native people experience cultural changes sweeping across the landscape.

The Mississippi period followed the Woodland and continued to 1700, about the time of widespread European contact. Within the Lower Mississippi Valley, social evolution resulted in ranked societies in which family of birth determined status. Chiefdoms were established, enabling control and direction of sizable labor forces that built hundreds of large, ceremonial mounds in the region. Around AD 1200 maize, a precursor of corn, had been traded into the area from the Southwest, eventually becoming an important food source that supported larger, sedentary populations. As the Mississippi period came to a close, native peoples lived in tribes that we came to know as Choctaw, Chickasaw, Tensas, Natchez, Ouachita, and Caddo. No large villages are known to have existed near the D'Arbonne Swamp, but the presence of vanished races here is beyond doubt in the remaining traces of seasonal campsites, eroded burial sites, scattered artifacts, and historical documents.

It is noteworthy that humans lived in the D'Arbonne Swamp area for twelve thousand years with negligible ecological impacts until Europeans arrived. In just one example of the changes since, pipeline and utility rights-of-way have altered the swamp more in the last fifty years than it changed in the previous twelve thousand years of habitation by Native Americans. Our European ancestors brought attitudes of Manifest Destiny to the wilderness, mindsets that hailed "progress" as justifiable regardless of cost to the natural world. We are yet laden with these postures in the twenty-first century.

I grew up on the south end of D'Arbonne Swamp just up the hill from the site of White's Ferry on the bayou. Within my pack of boyhood friends, a couple shared my wild fascination with Indian artifacts. We made countless expeditions along the banks of the bayou in search of the perfect arrowhead. On a good day I would find two, maybe three, and they were rarely perfect. In fact, I would learn many years later that few were actual arrowheads but rather dart or spear points or even small knife blades. And they weren't perfect in our eyes because most were crafted from local gravel instead of fine flints from Arkansas. Still, they lured us to the swamp, where we unwittingly began to learn the pieces and workings of forested wetlands. We discovered that the prime time to hunt arrowheads was soon after a headwater rise on the bayou scoured the banks of fallen leaves, and that it was useless to search on fresh sandbars because those surfaces were recently formed—elementary lessons in the science of hydrology. We never missed the opportunity to examine the exposed soil in the root-ball craters formed when strong winds toppled a huge willow oak. Here could be found the occasional incised potsherd, and someday we hoped to discover an actual intact vessel. We noticed that trails made by mink and raccoons often ringed the water-filled craters where crawfish dwelled, and that the seedling offspring of the fallen tree grew fastest where sunlight reached the ground—nascent examples of ecology. As it turns out, I wasn't the first in my family to ponder the swamp's early human inhabitants.

3

Clarence Moore and Great-Grandfather Rufus—
Indian Fish Traps—Swamp Consumers

Clarence Bloomfield Moore was born into a wealthy Philadelphia family in 1852. After graduating from Harvard, he traveled widely in Europe, Asia, and South America before returning home to run the family paper mill business on the death of his father in 1878. Clarence, or C.B. as he was known, secured his own fortune after a few years and set about devoting the rest of his life to his cherished avocation—archaeology. He became an archaeologist of sorts, at least in the science of the day. He roamed the Southeast plundering Native American mounds and burial grounds searching for artifacts, especially ornate pottery and bones. Many of his findings were eventually published in the *Journal of the Academy of Natural Sciences of Philadelphia*.

Moore's modus operandi was to ply the rivers and streams of the Southeast in his small, chartered steamboat *Gopher* with supplies and a crew of Black laborers. Months before his planned expeditions he would send out scouts to query local residents about the locations of mounds and other obvious archaeological sites. With potential areas to excavate in mind, he would depart on the *Gopher* when water levels were adequate to support navigation.

Shortly after New Year's Day in 1913, the *Gopher* pulled hard to port and entered the mouth of Bayou D'Arbonne from the Ouachita River above Monroe. The bayou was still years away from knowing the biodiversity-choking effects of locks and dams. Dusky and creole darters still lived in the gravel shoals that wagons could cross in late summer. It was winter now, and behaving as it should, the bayou left its banks and covered the flood-plain two miles wide between the red clay hills. Only the leafless crowns of overcup and willow oaks broke the surface of the adjacent flats. Understory water elms and mayhaws slept the season away completely submerged. The captain used the russet-feathered cypresses that lined the banks as channel markers.

One mile upstream the paddle-wheeler passed White's Ferry, closed for the season, and soon after churned over the drowned wreck of the *Rosa B.* In succession, local landmarks were washed in the boat's wake—Catfish Slough, Long Reach, Wolf Brake, Cross Bayou, Bayou Choudrant, Holland's Bluff, Eagle Lake, Old Mills, and finally the destination of the day—a spring-fed creek entering from the east known as Rocky Branch. Moore was looking for a man who owned land nearby and whose last name was spelled in part like the ancient word Ouachita. Moore had been informed by his scouts that evidence of aboriginal sites was located on the man's property. The man himself was reportedly an Indian.

Moore found the man, whose name was Rufus Ouchley. He was the patriarch of a local clan subsisting on the fruits of marginal soils and a fickle swamp. His background was clouded by time and suspicion of strangers. Of his ancestors little was known other than that his father, a private in the 31st Louisiana Infantry, was paroled at the fall of Vicksburg and walked back to this swamp.

Rufus led Moore to areas the family called the big and little Indian camps. Moore described them as humps and rises in a field near the bayou. The laborers dug into them, but the results disappointed Moore. They found no intact pots or burials, only broken potsherds, shells, fire-cracked rocks, and small, barbed dart points—worthless in the science of the day.

When questioned, Rufus had no knowledge of the former inhabitants of the Indian camps. He couldn't have. Later analysis of the grog- and shell-tempered pottery from the site would reveal the occupants to be members of the Coles Creek and Plaquemine cultures that flourished between 1,200 and 600 years ago.

The drama of the scene on this day was unappreciated by the players. A Harvard scholar of European origin impatiently scurried about giving orders to men of African descent in the name of science and glory. Ghosts of an American race long vanished drifted among the adjacent cypress trees. My great-grandfather stood barefoot in his fallow cornfield somewhere in the middle of a cultural stew. He could no more imagine the lives of the other actors than he could have that of a future great-grandson who would write of the historical episode on a computer only a few hundred yards from the site. Moore's report for his visit reads:

> The Ouchley Place, belonging to Mr. R. Ouchley, who lives upon it, is about one-half mile back from Bayou D'Arbonne, at a place where it is joined by Rocky Branch bayou.
>
> Part of the Ouchley Place is a large field along the side of which nearest the bayou are a number of humps and rises. Some of these were dug into by us unsuccessfully, the soil being without evidence of having served as dwelling-sites to any great extent. On the surface of these slight elevations, with one exception, was midden debris in small quantities, and it is probable the sites had served as places of abode for short periods or that the midden material had been washed away.
>
> One small hump had, superficially, considerable debris, including a number of small, barbed arrowpoints of flint. This rise was dug into with special care, and black soil showing former occupancy was found to a depth of about one foot. No burials were encountered.

Continuing upstream on the *Gopher,* Moore investigated four other locations on Bayou D'Arbonne at Turkey Bluff, Johnson Landing, Ruggs Bluff, and the Scott Place. Other than several mounds on the Scott Place, he found nothing that he considered important. However, because the bayou water level was high, he literally floated over two archaeological sites even rarer than mounds in Louisiana.

Native Americans were masters at exploiting the natural resources of their environment whether in southwestern deserts or southern swamps. Fish were highly desirable sources of protein as evidenced by their remains in hundreds of archaeological sites. Techniques for obtaining fish ran the gamut from hook and line, woven seines, and poisons from wild plant materials such as green walnut hulls. Especially in the eastern half of the United States, Indians devised another method to trap fish in shallow, flowing streams, by building V-shaped rock dams or weirs. The structures funneled fish into a small opening at the point of the V where a box trap often made of cane or hickory laths secured the fish. People would sometimes splash and drive their prey into the trap. Remains of these sites are scattered across many eastern states. A 1705 account from Virginia describes the process:

> At the falls of the Rivers, where the Water is shallow, and the Current strong, the Indians use another kind of Weir thus made. They make a Dam of loose stone where of there is plenty on hand, quite across the River, leaving One, Two or more Spaces or Tunnels, for the water to pass thro': at the Mouth of which they set a Pot of Reeds, Wove in form of a Cone, whose Base is about Three Foot, and in Perpendicular Ten, into which the Swiftness of the Current carries the Fish, and wedges them in fast, that they cannot possibly return.

A key element for building fish weirs was the presence of stones near a flowing stream, scarce items indeed in Louisiana's alluvial deposits of sand and clay. Until recently, the closest I have been able to sift from the literature was a weir discovered in south Mississippi in association with remains of split-cane netting thirty to forty feet long. The site was dated to AD 1460. Then, searching an old map with a magnifying glass, I found evidence of such structures in Louisiana barely three miles as the fish crow flies from my house on the edge of the swamp.

The US Army Corps of Engineers' first presence of substance on Bayou D'Arbonne occurred when Congress authorized a survey of the stream to determine the scope of "improvements" needed to enhance steamboat navigation. The work resulted in the first comprehensive survey, with accompanying maps titled "Map of Bayous D'Arbonne and Corney, Louisiana," dated September 1883. The maps are remarkable in detail, but some of the labels are so tiny as to be almost illegible without magnification. My closer look revealed a V-shaped mark pointing downstream identified as "Fish-trap Dam" in a shoal just below the mouth of Francis Creek. Farther up, below Crawford's Bluff, another was labeled "Old Fish Dam." The official report of Assistant Engineer F. S. Burrowes is even more revealing: "Twenty-two and a half miles above the mouth [of the bayou] Francis Creek enters the right bank, at the mouth of which the wreck of the steamer *Bertel Bruner* lies partly in the channel, and one-half mile farther down the channel is again obstructed by a stone dam 5 feet in height, built [to] hold a fish trap."

Both dams were in very shallow parts of the bayou, one foot deep according to the survey soundings. Both were located where uncommon outcrops of hematite surface and provide stones for construction. Although it is likely that settlers refurbished and re-used the fish traps as documented in other areas, they were almost certainly first built by people with hundreds of generations of expertise in such matters. Imagine the scene on a hot summer day as a dozen Indians young and old splashed, shouted, and laughed as they beat the water with canes to drive catfish, freshwater drum, and smallmouth buffalo into the trap on Bayou D'Arbonne. The thrill of fishing is ageless.

It is no exaggeration to say that beginning with the first non-native explorers most people of European heritage came to this region to exploit natural resources for personal gain. The pursuits, continuing through their ancestors to this day, involve consumptive uses of various living and abiotic resources, none of which has proven to be infinite. General apathy or ignorance of this simple element of our historic and current economic system hinders conservation efforts aimed at achieving healthy, sustainable lifestyles in perpetuity.

The ramblings of explorer Hernando de Soto's expedition in the Lower Mississippi Valley in the 1540s were a quest for gold. He didn't find any. Although his men's exact route in this region is speculative, there is a good chance that they passed through the Ouachita River watershed. Afterward, more than a century passed until the late 1600s when French-Canadian trappers drifted downstream to this region in pursuit of pelts from fur-bearing mammals. They were followed by more French hunters, traders, and a few settlers from the Pointe Coupee area of south Louisiana. Control of the area shifted from France to Spain and back to France again before the region became part of the United States with the Louisiana Purchase of 1803.

The first settlement near the D'Arbonne Swamp can be traced to 1785 at Prairie des Canots on the east bank of the Ouachita River six miles below the mouth of the bayou. It was soon called Fort Miro, a reference to

the Spanish fortification there of the same name. Growth of the community continued after the Americans took over in 1803, and in 1819 the first steamboat, the *James Monroe,* appeared before the hamlet. Excited citizens promptly changed the name of their village to Monroe, in honor of the boat, which was itself named for the president. Monroe later became the seat of Ouachita Parish.

Settlement in Union Parish was slightly behind that of Ouachita. John Honeycutt Sr. likely became the first permanent resident before 1795. By late 1797 he had sold his Spanish land grant, described as a "habitation with ten arpents frontage [on Bayou D'Arbonne] by the usual forty arpents depth," to Zadoc Harman, a man of African descent. Other records indicate the property was probably about a mile below the modern Lake D'Arbonne dam. In 1839 Union Parish was created from Ouachita Parish. Elected police jurors selected 160 acres near the confluence of Bayous D'Arbonne and Corney to become the parish seat. They named it Farmerville in recognition of Mills

Farmer, an early settler and veteran of the War of 1812. With the town of Monroe on the south end of the swamp and Farmerville on the north, several small communities cropped up in between as settlers from eastern states poured into the region prior to the Civil War. Their livelihoods continued to depend on consumption of natural resources. Those resources now included verdant forests and rich soils.

4

Cypress Trees—Backward Thinking—Bayou Steamboats

Nothing characterizes a southern swamp more than a giant, moss-draped cypress tree standing knee-deep in a backwater slough. Technically known as baldcypress (*Taxodium distichum*), these survivors of ancient life forms once found across North America and Europe are now greatly restricted in range. In the United States they are native to river bottoms and swamps in the Deep South and along the eastern seaboard north to Delaware. In Louisiana, although the last large virgin stands are gone, cypresses can still be found in every parish. In the D'Arbonne Swamp, cypresses formerly lined the channels of the bayou and grew in depressions in nearly pure stands called "brakes."

Cypress trees once grew to 17 feet in diameter and 140 feet in height. They were the largest trees in the South and lived to be four hundred to six hundred years old. A few were estimated to be more than a thousand years old. Even though cypresses are at home in wetlands, their seeds cannot germinate underwater and young seedlings soon die if they are overtopped by floodwaters during the growing season. Older trees can adapt to intermittent flooding regimes and usually develop fluted trunks, but permanent deep flooding will eventually kill most mature trees.

Historically, cypresses have always been important to humans wherever they grow. The reddish heartwood of old trees is durable and resistant to decay in a climate that fosters the rapid decomposition of most woods. For thousands of years Native Americans used cypress for dugout canoes. Early colonists were quick to discover its value as a building material. In 1797, Don Juan Filhiol described Fort Miro, the first sizable colonial structure in the

Ouachita Valley, as "an enclosure in post of tipped cypress . . . in an area [in] which is found the principal house . . . covered in cypress shingles." In the late 1800s the demand for cypress lumber for boats, furniture, pilings, trim, shingles, siding, and coffins was great. It was during this period that the vast virgin stands were logged over. By 1925 the once-thriving cypress industry was in a spiraling decline as the last of the raw products were exhausted.

Most cypress stands today are second or third growth, including those in the D'Arbonne Swamp, but there still remain a few giants among us, towering a hundred feet above the earth. They exist because they are hollow and thus not merchantable or because they grow in an area so remote as to make harvest unfeasible. They laid down their first annular rings during the classical period of the Mayan culture. They germinated and grew into seedlings as Charlemagne was crowned Holy Roman Emperor. They were sound and mature when the sun gleamed from the swords of Hernando de Soto's men as they marched across land that became northeastern Louisiana in a fruitless search for gold. It is possible that their limbs were once laden with the weight of a thousand passenger pigeons and that their bark was probed by ivory-billed woodpeckers. Cougars and bears may have sought refuge in their hollows. For the present, a few of these still greet each spring with a fresh feathering of needle-like leaves. If only we could interpret their soft murmurings . . .

On this place where my wife, Amy, and I live and that we call Heartwood, Rocky Branch flows intermittently throughout the year. In the last few thousand years this stream has carved a flat bottom two hundred yards wide in its meandering rambles through the red clay hills on its way to Bayou D'Arbonne. With the shallow water table beneath its watershed now depleted, the creek bed is often bone dry during the dog days of summer. However, the entire bottom may be inundated ten feet deep during naturally occurring spring backwater floods. It is a tentacle of the D'Arbonne Swamp.

By any measure, legal or otherwise, the bottom is a wetland. The soil is saturated for much of the growing season and water-tolerant plants grew there historically. Some, like cypress trees, still do. However, in this species and on this site lies a troubling mystery. Throughout the part of the bottom that is on our property about fifty medium-sized cypresses are scattered about. At

BALDCYPRESS
(Taxodium distichum)

some point in the past they were girdled all around with an axe. I'm guess-
ing this offense occurred forty to fifty years ago. Scar tissue has now grown
over the injuries where the vital cambium cells were hacked away, but the
trees still struggle to survive and likely haven't grown much since the assault.

What happened here? During the heyday of the cypress logging industry, which had crashed by the 1930s, large cypresses were sometimes killed by girdling and allowed to remain standing for a year so they would dry out and thus float when they were cut down. Corralled into large rafts, they could then be floated down to streamside sawmills. This could have been the intent of the Rocky Branch axman, but it seems a poor fit. The trees weren't large by cypress standards, and they seem to have been girdled long after local sawmills shut down. I'm leaning toward another scenario, one that involves the government and a different kind of tree that shouldn't even be growing in the bottom—loblolly pines. About the time the cypresses were girdled, the landowner in that day harvested many of the bottomland oaks and some large cypresses on the tract. Stumps remain as evidence of this activity. Soon afterward, off-site loblolly pines were planted throughout the area because they were fast-growing and more valuable than hardwoods. I've found records showing the former landowner was provided financial incentives through US Department of Agriculture programs to convert what was considered worthless swampland to a productive tree farm. It seems logical that the remaining smaller cypresses were girdled to prevent them from shading out the pine seedlings.

With fifty years of hindsight since the bungled attempt to kill the cypress trees, a number of ecological lessons could be taught using this anecdote. The pines have not thrived because they were planted in a wetland where they are not adapted to grow. They are shorter than normal and more disease-prone. They take up space where important wetland trees could be growing. Ironically, had the landowner encouraged the regrowth of native hardwoods and cypresses after his harvest, the forest would be much more valuable today from an economic as well as ecological perspective. Wanton girdling of cypress trees is not so much a tragedy as a reminder that the mechanisms of nature cannot be ignored.

Heaven knows early steamboats were a disruption to centuries of tranquility on the placid bayou. Alive with mechanical groans and shrieks, churning waterfalls in the quiet pools, belching embers like a lightning-struck, cypress chimney, they were alien creatures on the D'Arbonne. Record of the first such boat to make the hazardous, snag-studded trip up the bayou has yet to surface, but regular service to Farmerville began in 1848. By then the state of Louisiana had funded a project to remove the most serious obstructions in the channel. Even so, the captains were at the mercy of drastically fluctuating water levels and could only work the bayou several months a year. Because the channel was tortuous in its meanderings across the floodplain, steamboats by necessity were small in order to navigate the sharp bends and to turn around for outbound trips. Most were about 100 feet long and 24 feet wide and capable of hauling 400 bales of cotton. Since much larger boats could traverse the Ouachita River, the small steamers sometimes offloaded or picked up bayou freight at landings in Trenton near Monroe or at the mouth of the D'Arbonne.

The Civil War stymied steamboat commerce in the South, as many boats were pressed into Confederate military service or captured by Union forces. After the war, business on the bayou grew with the surrounding population. Landings were established at Holland's Bluff, Mosely's Bluff, Farmerville, and farther up Corney Bayou. Significant figures in the local steamboat trade included Thomas Rabun, William Wentzell, Daniel Stein, Lazarus Brunner Jr., and H. W. Vaughn. Following an 1883 detailed survey of the bayou by the US Army Corps of Engineers, a federal contract was issued to systematically clear the channel of remaining snags and other impediments. At the same time slips were dredged into the banks at landings to facilitate turning the steamboats around. Accordingly, the boats got larger. The *Bertha Brunner,* built in Cincinnati and specifically designed to work Bayou D'Arbonne, could carry a thousand bales of Union Parish cotton down to the Ouachita River in the first leg of a journey to New Orleans. Before the steamboat era came to a close, dozens of boats worked the D'Arbonne. Notable ones include *Oddity, Timmie Baker, Rosa B, Fair Play, Lind Grove, Poplar Bluff, Sterling White, Friendly, Mattie, Helen Vaughn, Tributary,* and *Belle of D'Arbonne.*

During the second half of the nineteenth century, local business leaders at both ends of the swamp touted the progress made in "taming" the bayou for economic interests involving steamboat commerce. But the fate of many D'Arbonne boats would remind local citizens that steamboats were still a risky business. Among the victims:

Oddity—1873; burned with cargo of 500 bales of cotton 8 miles above mouth of D'Arbonne.
Bertha Brunner—1879; grounded with 775 bales of cotton and burned in bayou at mouth of Francis Creek.

Rosa B—1881; "the best Bayou D'Arbonne boat ever built," burned with cargo of 800 bales of cotton 3 miles above mouth of D'Arbonne; loss of one life.

Fair Play—1881; burned at Monroe wharf; loss of one life.

Lind Grove—1884; burned at Monroe wharf.

Tributary—1890; burned with cargo of 300 bales of cotton at Turkey Bluff on the bayou. (The remains of this boat settled in a sharp bend of the bayou just downstream from the mouth of Rocky Branch. The site, known as "The Wreck," is prominent in my family lore.)

Helen Vaughn—1895; burned with cargo of 450 bales of cotton at White's Ferry on the bayou.

Cotton was not the only commodity shipped down the bayou on steamboats. One source lists the *Bertha Brunner* arriving in New Orleans in April 1875 with a cargo from Union Parish consisting of 128 bales of cotton, 1,600 barrel staves rived from local timber, and 118 head of livestock. Merchandise flowed upstream with the returning boats. Mail and freight, mostly via New Orleans, were offloaded at the various D'Arbonne landings. Wealthier customers received crates of iced oysters fresher than those in today's local markets and fine cloths from Europe. Yeoman farmers picked up staples such as flour and coffee, and necessities like plow harnesses and mosquito netting. Before the development of all-weather roads, steamboats also served as an important mode of transportation for passengers.

Railroad service reached Farmerville in 1904. From that time forward steamboat commerce began a steady decline as the trains were more dependable, faster, and competitive in freight costs. By 1920 the bayou was quiet again with only the occasional putt-putting of the small "gas boats" drifting across the flats of the adjacent swamp.

The decline of steamboat traffic was not lost on Rufus Ouchley. He had moved from the west side of the bayou near Point along with his bachelor brother, James (Uncle Jimmy), after they purchased 360 acres just up the hill from the mouth of Rocky Branch in February 1907. Rufus homesteaded there and with his wife, Lula, raised eight children by farming marginal soils and gathering resources from the often-grudging swamp. Always struggling to feed his brood of kids, he bought one of the first gas-powered boats on the bayou and rigged it up as a store boat in a business venture aimed at filling, at least in a small way, the vacant niche left by the steamboats. When ris-

Dogtrot House

ing spring water levels permitted, he would take orders in the community, corral my teenage grandfather as a mate, and steer the boat down to the general merchandise establishments in Monroe. After filling specific orders he bought staples and hardware to sell from his own store, little more than a shed near the dirt road in front of his dogtrot house. The venture did not lead to wealth, but his children did not go hungry. I suspect also for this man who could barely write his name that he derived satisfaction merely by looking at the letterhead on his order tablet of 1918: "R. Ouchley Dealer in General Merchandise Colsons, La."

5

Chains and Webs—Donnie—Illegal Activities

It is not possible to know if Rufus contemplated his place in the natural world consisting of the bayou and its swamp environs. The modern field of ecology has its own bag of words and terms used to describe the relationships between plants and animals and their environment. Food chain is one such term. Most folks grasp the basic meaning as "the big fish eats the little fish," which is pretty much the simplified truth. A more thorough definition might be a "chain of organisms in a community through which energy is transferred." An ecological community consists of the plants and animals living in a particular habitat. Each animal link in the chain obtains energy by feeding on the link below it, and in turn passes the energy on when it is eaten by the next link. A chain typically begins with a green plant (a producer) that gets its energy from the sun and proceeds through herbivores and then carnivores (consumers). Along Bayou D'Arbonne, a chain might begin when submerged willow roots on a sandbar are eaten by a crawfish, which then falls prey to an alligator snapping turtle whose destiny ends in a sauce piquant at the Baptist church's annual wild game dinner. Since every living organism is a link, there are many food chains in a community. Cumulatively, all of these food chains comprise a food web in a given area.

Energy is not the only thing that passes through food chains and circulates within the strands of a food web. Contaminants and pollutants, if present in the environment, often tag along for the ride and become more concentrated in each successive link of the chain. The process almost led to the demise of bald eagles when levels of DDT became so elevated in adult birds that reproductive failure ensued until the pesticide was banned. In the Bayou D'Arbonne watershed and surrounding area, mercury poison advisories are ubiquitous for some fish, usually large, predaceous species at the hot end of the food chain. Globally, oceans are being swamped with an estimated 600,000 tons of plastic microfibers annually from a variety of sources, and plankton at the critical lower end of the marine food chain are eating them. Their journey in time up through the links of "little fish and bigger fish" and finally into humans is a logical progression.

Within the broader scope of this topic, however, the greatest danger to our species is for the majority to get out of bed every morning oblivious to the fact that each of us is an inescapable link in a multitude of chains comprising a myriad of webs. Our well-being is welded hard to the health of the others. It is also worth noting that in the big picture, ours is the only unnecessary link.

In this narrative the name of a unique individual will surface from time to time—"Donnie." As a boy and still to this day, I think of him as "My Most Unforgettable Character" in the manner of *Reader's Digest* classics. His mother was the half-sister of my great-grandfather Rufus. He was of my father's generation and one of his lifelong friends. I can't remember when I did not know him. Larger than life, rougher than a corduroy road, he was scarred from battles in the south Pacific, local juke joints, and Hurricane Audrey in 1957. He was a profoundly creative curser and at least in the second half of his life wiser as a high school dropout than most academic scholars I know. He radiated Thoreau's exclamation, "How sweet is the perception of a new natural fact!" Donnie grew up in a clapboard house about a hundred yards from where I have lived for thirty years. The house is long gone, and he is also. What remains are his stories of growing up and just surviving on the edge of the D'Arbonne Swamp during the Great Depression through World War II. They likely represent typical experiences of many people in this place in those times. Over the years I wrote some down in spiral-bound notebooks.

—Donnie came by today, brought yard eggs, stayed a while, and talked of old times. He said his mother made him gather jimson weeds from the cow lot, dry it, and keep it on hand for people who had respiratory issues such as asthma. The leaves would be dried and smoked in a corncob pipe to give immediate relief to asthma symptoms. The plant was otherwise considered very poisonous.

—Donnie told water well stories on this day. He told about a well caving in on him while he was cleaning it out where my grandfather once lived. He spoke of the hazards of natural gas that accumulated in the hand-dug wells when they were working in them. He said they would often lower a candle or kerosene lamp into the well that would indicate danger if it went out.

—Donnie visited this evening, brought fresh smoked sausage and turnips. He said his brother Charles paid for this land (their old home place then, and ours that we call Heartwood now) twice, and he paid for it once when their dad mortgaged it to pay hospital bills. He said Charles paid for it by cutting pipeline rights-of-way with a crosscut saw. Donnie told about making a cotton crop that brought $30 profit at the end of the year. He said he bought a cotton dress for his sister and other clothes for his family with the money.

If there is a gene that enhances the propensity to enjoy fishing and hunting, I inherited the dominant allele for that trait. At the age of thirteen during the week of Thanksgiving I first killed a deer, illegally. The incident occurred at a place we call Old Mill in the D'Arbonne Swamp. Even then nothing remained of the former groundhog sawmill to distinguish the place from other overcup oak flats and cypress sloughs in the seasonally flooded swamp. Winter backwater had not yet topped the bayou bank to inundate our favorite hunting grounds and force us to the nearby red clay hills. My father grew up nearby, but deer were not found in this place when he was a boy. Extirpated locally by overhunting many years ago, the new herd resulted from restocking efforts by the Louisiana Department of Wildlife and Fisheries. Most originated in the vast Tensas Swamp, but some were brought in from Wisconsin, purportedly to improve the genetics of local deer and grow larger animals. Now the recently reopened season was short and only antlered bucks were legal game.

Plans for the day began long before sunrise in great-aunt Lillian's kitchen over plates of fried yard eggs, sausage, and biscuits with mayhaw jelly. The men decided where the hounds would be loosed and the positions of standers hopeful of intercepting quarry. After breakfast cousin Freddy and I were sent to the howling cacophony of the hound pens to fetch Popeye, Queenie, and others for the morning hunt. We leashed the bawling, long-legged Walkers with doubled-up hay strings, barely controlling their enthusiasm until we could pack them into a wooden crate in the back of an old Chevy pickup. They were to be released at a predetermined site after the standers were on location and followed by my great-uncle on his spirited, black and white paint stallion. I can now imagine the visage of Uncle Tony, hunting horn strapped over his shoulder and lever-action carbine across his lap as he rode straight-backed on the great horse, embellishing the cover of a nineteenth-century *Harper's Magazine.* In the predawn darkness with flickering flashlights, our small party of standers, comprised of my father, Donnie, and a few cousins of varying degrees, walked two miles into the swamp and took positions along known or suspected deer trails. Mine was beside a big willow oak on an outside bend of the bayou at Old Mill.

At first light, Uncle Tony released the frenzied hounds near Round Brake. His job was to rally the dogs until they jumped, to follow them on the horse during the chase, and head them off when possible if the deer decided to swim the bayou. Meanwhile, as hopeful standers, our emotions varied with the volume and proximity of the crying pack. Are the dogs coming this way or did they backtrack across Long Slough? Is the quarry just an old barren doe or the heavy antlered buck with drop tines that my cousin Michael missed last year on the ammonia pipeline?

Until mid-morning, the hounds cold-trailed nearly out of hearing, and I was getting bored. Then without warning five deer, all does, came bounding through the thickets, left to right, forty yards in front of me. The first round from my hand-me-down, single-shot, 20-gauge shotgun was a flock shot with no obvious impact on the herd. The shell extractor on the old gun was broken so I always carried a long, green stick to jam down the barrel to remove the spent shell. After this procedure I looked up to see a single doe standing in front of a large log. I cocked the hammer, fired again, and she jumped over the log out of sight. Trembling with excitement, I walked down the old logging trail toward Pasaw Island where I met my father and told him of the situation. Having heard the shots, Uncle Tony rode up on the stallion, which was stamping and blowing in the cold morning air. He rode back to investigate, returning soon to say that he had found the dead deer. The hunt continued, another doe was killed, and we walked out of the swamp at noon. That evening under the cover of darkness, Uncle Tony hauled the deer out on his horse. When he returned to the barn behind his house, I saw in the lantern light the deer I had shot for the first time since morning. Although there was no open season on antlerless deer in those days, I had been told in the past that I could shoot a doe if the opportunity arose, but I had been specifically warned against doing so on this morning because strangers were known to be hunting in the vicinity. Regardless, everyone seemed pleased that I had shot my first deer.

Memories of this event stuck, as did scenarios of grown men arguing over the proper way to hang a deer for skinning—head up or head down. Or of the image of my father walking down the highline toward me with snow on the ground and the legs of a deer hanging out each side of his hunting coat. Or of toting burlap sacks full of chopped sweet potatoes to Wolf Brake to illegally bait wood ducks that never came.

At that time, in the early 1960s, a conservation ethic did not exist in the general populace of the Deep South (or elsewhere in this country, I'm sure); the notion was that wildlife was there for the taking, not unlike dewberries or mayhaws in the swamp. These attitudes had been brought to North America by Europeans, a lingering remnant of Manifest Destiny. The state of affairs was exacerbated by a legal system hobbled with weak statutes and that did not take violations of natural resource laws seriously anyway. Posted property was uncommon. Stock laws did not exist in the D'Arbonne Swamp; hogs and cattle belonging to nearby farmers roamed the area to the detriment of wildlife. Aldo Leopold and a handful of like-minded associates were the only people of stature defining and touting the necessity of conservation tenets at landscape scale. Most of us then just did not think.

Many years later when I became manager of the national wildlife refuge that now encompasses a majority of the D'Arbonne Swamp, it occurred to me that most of my early memories of the area involved consumptive uses—activities that consumed natural resources of the bayou and swamp. Whether trapping raccoons for high school spending money, setting trotlines for catfish in spring backwater, or gathering muscadines for autumn jelly, I didn't appreciate the bounty I was reaping from the swamp. My activities as an individual were sustainable then, but times have changed. Now with the paint still drying on my bigger 3-D picture, it is these early memories that ensures my gratitude for the treasures that remain.

Well over a half century has drifted by Old Mill since I killed the doe. In that time such examples of fish and wildlife exploitation have decreased across the country, though they are still common enough and always will be. In Louisiana swamps the more egregious violations, including gross over-limits of waterfowl, shooting wood duck roosts, and market hunting, have declined significantly. The change is a factor of environmental education efforts in schools and by various conservation organizations. A maturing media has helped. The evolution of public opinion has carried over to the courts. There the status of wildlife crimes has been elevated, and penalties for violations are now severe enough to serve as effective deterrents. Changing the behavior of individuals, regardless of the technique employed (i.e., proactive education or punitive mandate), has been the key to reducing exploitation.

6

Enforcing the Laws—Bad Examples—Backwater—
Swamp Oaks—Removing the Forest

After a year or so of wandering in the wilderness of intermittent employment even while carrying a freshly minted graduate degree in Wildlife and Fisheries Science from Texas A&M University, I found happiness and a steady paycheck at the recently established Felsenthal National Wildlife Refuge (NWR). Encompassing sixty-five thousand acres of the Felsenthal Swamp and surrounding uplands, the refuge is bisected by the Ouachita River in Arkansas down to the Louisiana state line. It was only thirty miles from my home on the edge of another swamp where D'Arbonne National Wildlife Refuge was being created at the same time. At Felsenthal NWR the new manager was Charles Strickland, who had spent much of his career working in the Alaskan wilderness. He was a 6'3" redheaded, no-nonsense character with intentions of quickly bringing order to his new domain, especially as it related to the populace's reputation of blatant disregard of fish and wildlife laws. Taking a chance on me and Larry King, a young local schoolteacher, Charles called us into his office in the autumn of 1978 and declared something in the order of "Consider yourselves hereby sworn in to enforce all applicable Federal fish, wildlife, and other public use regulations in this neck of the woods." Along with tarnished badges for identification, he handed us each an old, military surplus, Smith & Wesson .38 Special revolver stamped "US Navy" on the butt. The worn leather holsters were right-handed and I am not. My partner's background in terms of consumptive use of resources was similar to mine; we had abandoned our "old ways" a few

years earlier, and we loved our new charge. This was a starting point of my duties as a National Wildlife Refuge officer that lasted until I retired from the US Fish and Wildlife Service more than thirty years later. The law enforcement duties were "collateral," meaning they were in addition to my other obligations as a biologist and refuge manager. The law enforcement experiences, many in the D'Arbonne Swamp, were at various times exciting, boring, sad, and hilarious. In the realm of officer safety, typical law enforcement encounters do not exist. Whether the incidents were minor or serious, everyone involved usually learned from these encounters.

On the morning of December 20, 1987, waterfowl hunting season was ongoing, and I was prowling about in search of violators. Before daylight I walked a mile into a swampy, forested area of oak flats and cypress sloughs. Palmetto blanketed the subtle ridges. Drapes of Spanish moss hung motionless in the still, predawn darkness. I squatted down and leaned back against a cedar elm to await the morning chorus. There was no sunrise on this cloudy day; objects just grayed into existence. Crows got up first and shouted insults at each other as they flew east toward the river. A pair of pileated woodpeckers were roused from their separate roosts and rattled greetings back and forth across the swamp. A tiny winter wren twittered from a nearby hollow log. As wood ducks began to fly over at treetop height, squealing their high-pitched cries, I figured they would soon reveal the presence of any hunters in the area. Sure enough, shotgun volleys abruptly splintered the natural sounds of the swamp.

From the sound of the shooting there appeared to be two hunting parties several hundred yards apart. They continued to fire intermittently for a while until the morning flight of ducks tapered off. I had a hunch which direction they would leave the area and moved to intercept them to conduct a routine field check. About 8:30, according to my field notes, I saw two hunters walking through the woods directly toward me. They turned out to be a man and his juvenile son. Not long after I had conducted my business with them and sent them on their way, I saw two more hunters approaching. In a similar scenario, they were also a man and his young son.

The encounters were not unusual except for several coincidences that bound them in my memory. Both men had the same last name except for the spelling by one letter. Both were from Shreveport but later claimed to have not met before the previous evening when they stayed at a nearby hunting camp. Each father and son collectively exceeded the daily bag limit of ducks. In each case the father claimed to have shot the "extra" ducks although the sons carried those birds when confronted. As I wrote citations for the men and seized the birds for evidence, it occurred to me that the boys were about the age of my own two sons. Old recollections stirred in me, and I remember it being hard not to preach to the men. Months later in court they expressed remorse at their behavior in the presence of the boys. I have often wondered if things changed afterward between the men and their sons, if their bond was altered, if maybe a lasting conservation ethic surfaced for all of them in the wake of the incident. I know the latter is possible, as I am my own example of youthful reformation.

Few people outside the Lower Mississippi Valley (LMV) can relate to the term "backwater" like those who live near the D'Arbonne Swamp. It refers to the natural, cyclic overflow of rivers and bayous that inundates areas characterized by bottomland hardwood vegetation. Backwater generally occurs in winter or spring in response to heavy seasonal precipitation on local watersheds or as far away as the upper tributaries of the Mississippi River. The key word in this definition is "natural" because backwater has created much of the land that we know here and continues to shape the flora and fauna.

Backwater dictates the type of plants that grow in overflow areas by replenishing shallow water tables to ensure that only species adapted to live in wetlands can survive. Pine seedlings frequently invade the D'Arbonne Swamp during dry cycles only to be killed when the floods return. The rising and falling waters disperse floating fruits and seeds of mayhaw, overcup oak, water hickory, and cypress to provide diversity throughout the ecosystem.

From longnose gar to largemouth bass, backwater is the key to many fisheries by providing critical spawning habitat. Backwater allows the temporary passage of fish from one oxbow lake to another, again ensuring diversity down to the genetic level. Native terrestrial wildlife have adapted to the floods. Some, such as squirrels and raccoons, can become completely arboreal for months in the D'Arbonne bottoms. Others, including deer, routinely follow the water in and out of the swamp as slowly rising waters cause few problems for most species if suitable habitat is available in nearby uplands. The most valuable function of backwater is likely the infusion of nutrients to fuel the system from the bottom up. Several million acres of former backwater areas in the Lower Mississippi Valley never or rarely flood because of levees, ditches, pumps, and dams. Most have been converted to agriculture. Even in remaining forested areas the cycle is broken, and the land is never as productive. Nutrient-deficient plants eventually produce less fruit, acorns, and browse, lowering the carrying capacity of the deer herd. Lack of flooding results in fewer fish and crawfish to support great blue herons, alligators, and otters. The absence of backwater means less seed and animal dispersal and thus less diversity. When diversity decreases to a finite point, ecosystems often implode and cease to exist as a sustainable unit.

For thousands of years humans adapted to backwater and even exploited its benefits without altering the natural phenomenon. Only in the last hundred years has man developed the tools to change the environment of the LMV at a landscape level. Backwater regimes still function in the D'Arbonne Swamp, but at some levels in some places we are progress poor.

Oaks are dominant tree species in bottomland hardwood forests. They can be divided into two major groups comprised of red oaks and white oaks. Those in the white oak group have leaves with rounded edges and acorns that mature in a single season. Examples of white oak types that grow in the D'Arbonne Swamp include overcup oak, delta post oak, and cow oak. Leaves of red oaks are usually bristle-tipped, and their acorns take two years to mature. Lowland species in the D'Arbonne Swamp are willow oak, water oak, cherrybark oak, and Nuttall oak. Willow oak and water oak are commonly called pin oaks locally, but true pin oaks don't occur naturally in the state and generally grow north of central Arkansas.

In natural settings oak trees are site-specific by species. Lowland oaks are tied closely to land elevation, hydrology, and soil type. Overcup oaks grow near the lowest, wettest areas in the swamp, just a bit higher than cypress. Moving upward in elevation, perhaps only a few inches, the oak component changes to willow oak and Nuttall oak. These in turn will be replaced by water oak and occasionally cherrybark oak as one progresses upward to the subtle ridges along the bayou and swamp edges.

Over thousands of years each species has adapted to grow best in specific conditions. Changes in these conditions, either natural or man-made, can prove devastating. A good example can be found along Bayou D'Arbonne, where hundreds of acres of willow oak have died in recent years. The die-off is tied to dams of the Ouachita River Navigation Project that raised water tables in the affected area. Trees, unable to adapt to the new, wetter site, were severely stressed, making them susceptible to natural diseases and insects. They succumbed en masse, leaving their long-term replacements as yet unpredictable.

More than 7 million acres of bottomland hardwood forests have been cleared and converted to agriculture in the Lower Mississippi Valley in the last century. Oaks were a primary component of this ecosystem and anchored the rich biodiversity. Every animal from bears to songbirds was tied directly or indirectly to oaks.

In recent years government conservation agencies have begun efforts to reforest some of the cleared areas that proved to be marginal farmland. Thousands of acres have been replanted to oaks and other native trees. The science of reestablishing naturally functioning bottomland forests is barely beyond infancy, but successes to date are encouraging and a sign that oak forests can be restored with public support.

The primeval forests of the D'Arbonne Swamp and environs are long gone, their quantitative dimensions and diversity hard to imagine today. The surveyor-explorer William Darby wrote in his 1816 Geographical Description of the State of Louisiana, "The Derbane [D'Arbonne] occupies the eastern slope of those hills. No prairies are found on this river; the whole extent from which its waters are drawn is a thick forest, composed of pine, oak, ash, hickory, linden, and almost every other forest tree found in the northern part of Louisiana. The pine occupies the hills and plains at a distance from the streams. Near the water courses many secondary bottoms or slopes are met with where the pine is found, admixed with oak, sweet gum and dogwood." Catharine Cole, an intrepid writer for the New Orleans *Picayune* attempted to describe them in an 1892 article:

It was within the boundaries of Union Parish I came upon a typical and true Louisiana forest. . . . The yellow, rutty country road twisted through it in a rustic fashion, and by the roadside were the . . . blood-red spears of Indian head, wild daisies and prim brown-eyed Susans, with late goldenrod, oaks, blackjack and the all but priceless white oaks. Here were beautiful beeches with their pale, mottled green and gray stems, flinging their airy foliage lightly in the wind, next to huge walnut and hickory trees, nut-laden, and now and again a dazzling holly or, prettier still, those graceful vestal virgins of the forest, the dogwoods, now all coraled over with seeds on their pale horizontal branches. Here too, were fragrant bays filling the air with incense, and magnolias whose fine-grained, ivory-colored fabric is so beautiful for interior decoration. Red oaks, ash and maple I found also in this Union forest, but loveliest of all were the sweet gum trees. They rivaled any pine in height, tall, slim gothic columns of foliated color, crimson, cherry-red, golden yellow or bronze. I saw five in a row delicately tapering to the skies.

For pioneering settlers it was a forested world that presented a paradox for all who struggled to make a life in this region. Vast stands of virgin timber along the Ouachita River and its tributaries were belligerent adversaries for prospective farmers armed only with axes and crosscut saws. They quickly learned not to waste their land-clearing labor in areas subject to the whims of backwater flooding, instead prematurely wearing out their mules and themselves on the high ground around the swamps. At the same time, they perceived the trees as a source of potential wealth beyond logs for their cabins and split rail fences. Markets in New Orleans and elsewhere clamored for the timber if only it could be delivered to their hungry sawmills. Options in the years following the Civil War were limited. Trees in the swamps were cut in the dry season and floated out to streams when the annual flooding occurred. There they were lashed together in rafts and floated downstream with the currents. The timbermen often camped on the rafts, riding them many miles to the ravenous mills before catching a ride home on a steamboat. In some cases, on rivers as large as the Ouachita, steamboats would tow the rafts to market. Bayou D'Arbonne was too wild in its meanderings to allow such maneuvers, and hiring a steamboat was a big expense for a small-scale logger.

With advances in technology and available capital, logging operations became more complex. Small, steam-powered, groundhog mills assembled in the forests sawed trees into rough lumber or barrel staves on-site. Products were then hauled by wagon to the nearest steamboat landing. The mills were frequently moved because all the nearby trees had been processed or because of seasonal flooding. One such mill was located on the bank of Bayou D'Arbonne three miles downstream from the mouth of Rocky Branch. The site is deep in the swamp and now flanked by an overcup oak flat. An 1883 report of the US Army Corps of Engineers states, "the ruin[s] of an old mill in the upper end of the section lie right in the channel." Circumstances leading up to the demise of the mill are cloudy. Perhaps it burned, or perhaps the bayou in the midst of a midnight storm shifted its course just enough to undermine the foundation. In any event, spring backwaters flooded the site ten feet deep in those times as well as today.

The place is well known in my family's topographic memory. We call it, appropriately, Old Mill, and it is laden with stories. Rufus said the owner was murdered by an unknown assailant, or at least one who was never prosecuted. The owner allegedly buried a large sum of money (likely gold, as is the custom of these tales) nearby. Rufus spoke of going to the mill site with a "mineral rod" to look for the treasure. He said the device alerted on a large sweetgum, which they cut into and found to be hollow. There was no gold and they concluded the detector went off because of "gas" trapped in the tree. Today the place looks like a thousand others in the D'Arbonne Swamp. It looked that way more than half a century ago when as a teenager I daydreamed of buried gold while waiting there to kill my first deer. The treasure still exists, but it is buried in the stories.

I digress. By the turn of the twentieth century, the barely tapped timber reserves of the region began to attract out-of-state lumber men who started buying large tracts of forest lands. Soon after 1900 the Union Saw Mill Company was created and eventually acquired 250,000 acres along sixty miles of the Ouachita River beginning in Arkansas and stretching downstream toward Monroe. A large sawmill was built at Huttig, Arkansas, followed by a railroad from that point to Monroe. The result was biota-altering forestry operations on an industrial scale that continue to dominate the landscape today. The process involved laying spur lines off the main railroad line into areas with abundant timber. Temporary logging camps housing up to two hundred men and their families, Black and white, were constructed along a spur line. The men felled and bucked trees and pulled them to loader sites with mules and oxen. There they were loaded onto massive wagons for transport to the nearest rail siding. A steam-powered loader on the train loaded the logs onto a long string of flatcars for transport to the mill at Huttig. As an area was cut out, the camps were moved, and the spur line rails were picked up and laid into a new stand of virgin trees.

For the D'Arbonne Swamp, a threnody of sledgehammers on steel spikes sounded during construction of a trestle across Bayou de L'Outre at the upper end of Hudson Lake. The new spur line provided direct access for exploitation of the swamp. Between 1912 and 1925 the bottomland forest was systematically removed, but it was not clear-cut. With no market for hardwood pulpwood, only the best sawlogs were cut, leaving low-grade hardwood timber and pulpwood. When the large lumber camps closed, logging activities reverted to small-scale operations and groundhog mills dependent on scrapping up leftovers of the virgin forests. During these times Rufus was known to push a small raft of logs down the bayou to Monroe with his new gas boat.

7

Wood Ducks—A Bay Horse and Outlaws—More on Squealers

I cannot choose just one favorite bird that inhabits D'Arbonne Swamp. You must allow me several. However, in the avian guild no species embodies the essence of a southern swamp more than the wood duck. Considered by many to be the most beautiful of North American waterfowl, wood ducks have been revered for centuries. Native Americans in the Lower Mississippi Valley commonly depicted wood ducks on pottery and ceremonial pipes. Their bones have been identified at numerous ancient sites of human habitation. The first Europeans here surely noticed the wood duck, and Cabeza de Vaca may have been the first to describe the species in his account of a bird he called the "royal drake" in 1527. By the seventeenth century wood ducks were exported to Europe and bred in captivity.

As is all too often the case, we damn near admired them to extinction. Having a reputation as gourmet table fare didn't help them. Nor did their habit of concentrating in large communal roosts at night, making them disproportionately vulnerable to market hunters and run-of-the-mill poachers. Unregulated hunting and to a lesser extent habitat loss sent populations plunging across most of the wood ducks' range in the early 1900s. They held on in remote forested wetlands such as D'Arbonne Swamp until passage of the Migratory Bird Treaty Act of 1918, when all wood duck hunting was prohibited. Legal hunting resumed in 1941 as populations recovered, but even though market hunting was eliminated as a serious issue, exceeding the daily bag limit of two birds several times over and hunting after legal shooting hours remained a critical problem.

WOOD DUCK (AIX SPONSA)

Shooting a wood duck roost is exciting in a thoughtless, primitive manner. During fall and winter wood ducks instinctively gather in large communal roosts sometimes numbering several thousand birds. For safety they choose dense thickets of flooded brush, often buttonbush in D'Arbonne Swamp, in which to spend the night. Just as darkness falls (and after legal shooting hours) they come swirling down from the evening sky in groups of five, ten, or twenty, hell-bent on landing in the chosen spot. Not even point-blank muzzle blasts of 12-gauge shotguns deter their mission. As every wood duck within several miles concentrates on landing in a roost often less than a half-acre in size in a matter of minutes, it is a frantic dissonance of whistling birds, rushing wings, splashing landings, and gunfire. Even poor marksmen kill birds in such situations, and many are never retrieved in the dark thickets. For too many of us, it was a rite of passage that was wrong. When my father was a young man, the behavior cost him two weeks' pay and missed work in a time when money and jobs were scarce. I was spared penalties for similar conduct during my adolescent antics only by grace and good fortune.

On the Saturday before Thanksgiving in 1991, I woke at 3:00 a.m. and drove to Catahoula Lake in central Louisiana, arriving well before daylight to assist Special Agent Joe Oliveros in the stakeout of a duck blind where, according to a tip, illegal numbers of ducks were being killed. As is sometimes the case in such law enforcement activities, uncertainties and confusion reigned while we tried to sort out the facts of the matter. Two vehicles matching the description of the subjects' truck appeared at separate boat ramps. Strong winds spawned whitecaps on the shallow lake at dawn, the hunters did not immediately launch their boats, and our several-hour surveillance ended up being for naught. In mid-afternoon Joe and I decided to save the issue for another day and headed our separate ways.

While I was driving home it occurred to me that I would pass within a few miles of a wood duck roost that I had discovered years earlier. Hoping for a productive ending to the day, I turned down a side road toward the Boeuf River Swamp as the sun approached the western horizon. About a mile from the roost I hid my unmarked vehicle in a thicket and leaned against the warm hood to listen. It occurred to me that in these times if an effective silencer was ever developed for shotguns, the illegal slaughter of waterfowl would increase exponentially because the roar of gunfire often exposes illicit behavior. The telltale shots on this evening began just as the wood ducks started flying in to the roost and just as legal hunting hours ended. I hurriedly drove to within a quarter mile of the shooting and pinpointed the source in a buttonbush slough bordered by a pasture. Scattered trees and a pair of horses provided the only cover as I slipped toward the hunters. Running and crawling at times, I wanted to get as close as possible to the outlaws before they detected me. The horses were a concern because I didn't want to spook them, which might alert the poachers, who were by now blasting away at the incoming birds. One horse, a big bay gelding with white fetlocks, spied me and began to amble in my direction. I continued on in the fading light until I could discern three armed men just a few yards away. By this time, fire was flashing from their barrels when they shot. In this tense situation and as I kneeled to record the times and volleys as evidence in my small notebook, the curious horse walked up to me and pressed his muzzle into the small of my back. Intent on my subjects, I was able to ignore him until he began gently pushing me forward. When he actually began to pick me up by my gun belt, I had had enough. "Whose side are you on?" I angrily hissed as I stood to face him. Tail high, he whirled and galloped away, farting and tossing his head as if this was some grand equine joke.

The men, occupied now with searching for the ducks they had killed and crippled in the thickets, didn't notice my frustrating episode with the horse. I contacted them when they walked into the edge of the pasture, then advised them to unload their guns and proceed back to their vehicle. One of the men, obviously the alpha male of the group, was belligerent and stated that had he chosen to do so, he could have easily outrun me and escaped. I responded that that was certainly possible, but for future reference he should know it would have then been necessary for me to seize his nice SUV with its attached trailer, two ATVs, and other equipment. By persistent probing, I determined that all three men had issues beyond the fact that they had violated federal law by shooting wood ducks after legal hunting hours. An ice chest on their trailer held three daily limits of ducks that they admitted to killing earlier in the morning. The birds they now possessed from the evening hunt were illegal lagniappe.

Several months later in federal court, the US magistrate judge considered the violations serious enough to warrant substantial fines and other penalties. Several years later at an outdoor sporting equipment show a man approached me and asked if I recognized him. I did not until he said he was one of the subjects in this case. To this day though, I'm quite sure I could pick the bay gelding with white fetlocks out of a lineup.

I knew wood ducks by the colloquial name "squealer" until wildlife biology professors convinced me of the value of using accepted taxonomic labels if I wished to advance in my chosen field of work. Their repertoire of squeals and whistles can be heard year-round in the swamp as resident birds are augmented by northern migrants beginning in late autumn until they venture northward again in late winter. A long-term banding program in the D'Arbonne Swamp has revealed fascinating information about their life history. In late summer biologists deploy rocket nets at baited sites to capture local wood ducks before northern birds arrive. The netted birds are tagged with numbered, aluminum bands and released. Data accrue when the banded birds are later shot by hunters (who report the harvest specifics to a national database) or recaptured by banders. Not surprisingly, most wood ducks banded in the D'Arbonne Swamp are recovered in Louisiana with many others showing up in Mississippi, Texas, and Arkansas. Some, however, are reported from most states in the eastern half of the United States and several Canadian provinces as well. A closer look at the data reveals that all wood ducks reported from locations farther north are males. Because birds pair up here in the swamp on their wintering grounds, this means that if a local D'Arbonne-born male chooses a Yankee mate while she is here for the winter, he will follow her home in the spring to breed there, be it Ohio or Ontario. Whether we call them squealers or wood ducks, the species is representative of how little we really know about the natural world.

In late winter courtship rituals begin in earnest for the resident wood ducks with females searching for suitable nesting sites. They are among a small group of waterfowl that nest in tree cavities and are often observed in "unducklike" positions as they walk along high limbs peering into nooks and hollows. Modern industrial forestry practices have eliminated conditions under which natural cavities develop in many areas as trees don't reach the age necessary to form cavities, and those that do are cut down as undesirable. Fortunately, wood ducks readily adapt to artificial nest boxes placed in suitable habitat. Throughout the refuge portion of D'Arbonne Swamp, cypress nest boxes have been erected to supplant natural cavities. Similar management activities and effective law enforcement have led to the recovery of the species throughout its range, and today's populations are healthy and secure. The simple fact that we have the ability to eliminate or nurture most life forms on this planet should sober us beyond apathy on such matters.

8

Bayou D'Arbonne Lake—Ode to an Overcup—Downstream Dams

For all practical purposes the upper quarter of the D'Arbonne Swamp was eliminated in 1957. In that year the Louisiana state legislature appropriated the first funds that led to the construction of Bayou D'Arbonne Lake. A year earlier the Bayou D'Arbonne Lake Watershed District Board of Commissioners had been created for "the conservation of soil and water, developing the natural resources and wealth of the district for sanitary, agricultural and recreational purposes." The applied objective of the board (which still exists) was to promote the lake project. With the support of local politicians and businessmen plugging economic development, the project moved forward. A site was chosen to dam Bayou D'Arbonne below Farmerville where the hills on both sides probed farthest into the swamp. Work began on the fifty-four-foot-tall dam in 1961. It consisted of an earthen berm on the west end and 2,450-foot concrete dam and spillway on the east side. When completed in 1963 at a cost of approximately $3 million, the lake soon filled to permanently flood 15,280 acres of the former swamp and adjacent uplands. Habitat for prothonotary warblers was converted to that of channel catfish.

From the beginning the lake was popular for fishing, boating, swimming, and water skiing. Fourteen public boat ramps were built along with a modern state park to facilitate camping, hiking, and other outdoor activities. Economic growth tied to lakeside housing and modest tourism has been realized. From a scenic perspective, the lake is beautiful. It is not, however, immune to conflicts between user groups. Starting with disputes between commercial and recreational fishermen over appropriate fishing

Bayou D'Arbonne Lake Dam

regulations, the quarrels now center on conflicting viewpoints of home-owners and fishermen as to how lake levels should be managed. Over the half-century life of the lake, homeowners progressively built closer to the lakeshore while ignoring the potential of natural flood events. Such willful disregard of normal, recurring incidents has resulted in extensive property damage at times. The subsequent outcry to harness nature, along with the usual threats of lawsuits, yielded a major modification to the dam in 2013. At a cost of $8.7 million, two tainter gates were built into the dam allowing much higher volumes of water to be released during floods. Many fisher-men are convinced rapid lake fluctuations are bad for fishing. Meanwhile, the board of commissioners struggles to appease everyone.

Ecologically, the dam converted the swamp to artificial lacustrine hab-itat. It eliminated the homes of inestimable numbers of terrestrial animals (mammals, birds, reptiles, and amphibians) not to mention native trees and other plants. In 1963, just before the lake filled, Dr. Robert Kral, a botanist from Vanderbilt University, collected six species of rare plants on a steep slope about four miles southwest of Farmerville:

Adiantum pedatum	Northern Maidenhair Fern
Hydrangea arborescens	Wild Hydrangea
Quercus rubra	Northern Red Oak
Saxifraga virginiensis	Virginia Saxifrage
Solidago hispida	Hairy Goldenrod
Woodsia obtusa	Blunt Woodsia

Within months the site was permanently flooded, and except for a few of the oaks, the plants have never been found here again. However, the dam greatly increased aquatic habitat for some freshwater fish, turtles, and a handful of bird species. Bald eagles and ospreys in particular are much more abundant now, and wintering water birds like common loons, ruddy ducks, and lesser scaup were absent before the lake. Though less dramatic, impacts of the dam are not limited to the bounds of the reservoir as they flow downstream through the remaining swamp. Natural pulses of water down the bayou were an integral factor in the life cycle of many species. They triggered spawning behavior in some fish, especially those tied to backwater flooding like buffalo and gar. They enabled seed dispersal by plants with evolved mechanisms to distribute their progeny via floating embryos. In the D'Arbonne Swamp this includes overcup oak and baldcypress. When the flow through the dam is regulated by humans with a plan that ignores downstream impacts, very unnatural events occur. Exacerbated by the tainter gates, tremendous volumes of water are released into the bayou in a short period of time, far exceeding the parameters of a natural pulse. Often the releases are unnatural in their timing as well. A lake drawdown is now scheduled every four years during the autumn, typically the driest time of year, "to allow for maintenance of shoreline properties and provide control of nuisance aquatic vegetation." In addition to unknown but certain impacts on native plants and animals, the results include severe channel scouring and streambank erosion. One has only to float the D'Arbonne for a mile or so to note dozens of large, fallen trees in the channel. Most have tumbled into the bayou from eroded banks in the last five years. Bank erosion and channel scouring, having occurred for thousands of years as the bayou meandered back and forth across its floodplain, are not new phenomena. As with ongoing global climate change, it is the rate of change that is unnatural. Just as the dammed lake is not natural, the remaining D'Arbonne Swamp is less natural because of the dam also (in spite of the bayou being a component of the Louisiana Natural and Scenic Rivers System). Across the southern landscape, there is no shortage of anthropomorphic lakes; the same can't be said of intact bottomland hardwood swamps.

Her days are numbered, and she won't likely last the winter. This prognosis is not arboreal soothsaying but rather the physics involved in supporting upright tons of wood fiber. Already she cants thirty degrees northwest and half her root system is embarrassingly exposed to all. Erosion, that hissing wave of gravity-fueled fluid that drags the main channel of the Mississippi River dozens of lateral miles across its floodplain like a writhing cottonmouth, works 24/7 on Bayou D'Arbonne also. A year ago, it broke the anchor chains of this overcup oak. Although with dying roots the tree has lost the ability to maintain intimate relationships with soil bacteria and fungi, interactions critical to her physical well-being, she managed to produce one last crop of acorns this year as notes of a fertile swansong. No oak is better adapted to live in swampy, flood-prone areas than overcup. Her parenchyma cells are closed to keep water out, a fact not lost on whiskey distillers who use the wood for barrels to keep spirits in. Closed cells may help overcups survive periods of frozen backwater. It is her acorns though that are most unique. Overcups are the only lowland oak species to produce viable acorns that float. What better way to distribute your offspring throughout a seasonally aquatic landscape?

The D'Arbonne oak was fortunate. She began life as an acorn perhaps forty feet from the bayou's edge. In the last century her acorn crops have been naturally sporadic depending on climate variables and the availability of nutrients. In the best of years, thousands of her acorns fell during autumn cold fronts and floated away on winter backwaters, a few lucky ones to land in sunlit harbors. All the while, the bayou crept closer to the parent tree.

When the tree falls, her uppermost branches will stretch two-thirds the distance across the bayou; even in death she will contribute to the swamp ecosystem. Bark and leaves along with the resurrection fern that homesteaded her cleavage will be swept away in spring freshets to become detritus for those tiny protozoans at the bottom of the food web upon which all other bayou life depends. Crappie will spawn in the protective cover of the treetop. The hollow trunk will provide habitat for flathead catfish and snapping turtles. When the bayou is at pool stage some of the limbs will protrude above the surface like witch's fingers—hunting perches for rattling kingfishers and patient anhingas. By then her last germinating acorns will be anxious seedlings struggling in the way of all life to take her place.

That the upper portion of D'Arbonne Swamp was transformed by a huge dam across the bayou is obvious; that the rest of the area was impacted by dams far removed from the swamp proper is alien to most casual observers. By the turn of the twentieth century the clamor to harness the nation's rivers in the name of economic progress was growing louder, and regional businessmen preached the virtues of taming the Ouachita River for the assured well-being of the local citizenry. Congressional representatives carried the message to Washington, where it was thrown into a grab bag with many others of like kind, the end result being authorization in 1902 of a minimum 6.5-foot-slack water channel on the Ouachita River via a lock and dam system. The dams scattered along the river were designed to guarantee sufficient water levels year-round for commercial vessels of the day. They were completed in 1925. The first dam on the river below the mouth of Bayou D'Arbonne backed water up the bayou unnaturally during low water periods. Impacts on the flora and fauna were likely minimal and limited to the lowest stretches of the bayou on a seasonal basis.

Commerce on Bayou D'Arbonne had long since yielded to the railroads, but the locks and dams did result in moderate barge traffic on the river in service to a few chemical plants, paper mills, and refineries. In keeping with the bigger-is-better mantra of economic development, especially if the government is picking up the tab, a new plan surfaced to provide a deeper channel that would enable larger barges to exploit the river for the new businesses that would surely arise. Hence in 1950, Congress authorized construction of a completely new set of locks and dams to increase channel depth to a minimum of nine feet. After further study of the Ouachita Navigation Channel Project, additional legislation in 1957 authorized building a large lock and dam upstream of Columbia, Louisiana. This became the

Columbia Lock & Dam

new dam that would impact Bayou D'Arbonne. Work began in 1964 and was completed in 1972. It backed water up the bayou at least twenty miles. While the new permanent flooding was not nearly as dramatic as that created by Lake D'Arbonne, even a few inches in a swamp can make a vital difference to resident plants and animals. Such was the case in the D'Arbonne Swamp. I first noticed changes on the bayou while on a visit home from college. The high White's Ferry Bridge, once a favorite platform for boys to jump into the bayou far below on a sizzling summer afternoon, was now closer to the water, even at pool stage.

The navigation project's potential negative impacts on fish and wildlife resources were recognized and debated during the planning process. Ultimately, the US Army Corps of Engineers (COE) agreed to purchase lands in two areas to be transferred to the US Fish and Wildlife Service (FWS) as mitigation for resource damage. Congress authorized these purchases for National Wildlife Refuges (NWRs) in the River and Harbor Act of 1970. They became Felsenthal NWR along the Ouachita River in Arkansas just above the Louisiana boundary and D'Arbonne NWR along Bayou D'Arbonne beginning 1.5 miles upstream from its confluence with the river. It is notable that the projected increase in river commerce never occurred with the latest locks and dams, and COE has since attempted to abandon the navigation project because of high maintenance costs. Only the regular pleas of local politicians keep it afloat. However, the National Wildlife Refuges have become oases for wild flora and fauna, as well as popular venues for outdoor recreation.

9

"Smallmouth Bass"—The Refuge—Mayhaws

Always in late February when the first white crawfish reached two inches in length a ritual took place in the D'Arbonne Swamp that included my father, his cousin Donnie, and me, an adolescent youth in those years a half-century ago. Our objective was to catch "smallmouth bass" for the deep, black skillet, but first we needed bait. Using a long-handled, homemade drag consisting of a joint of one-inch galvanized pipe attached to a basket of hardware cloth, we scraped the ditches along White's Ferry Road for the tender crawfish. When a sufficient number filled the steel, five-gallon bucket stuffed with Spanish moss, we were set to go the following morning. Barring a late cold front, we would launch the low-sided Arkansas Traveler at Holland's Bluff landing at first light as wood ducks beat their way from buttonbush roosts to the oak flats. The bayou was different then, before the Corps of Engineers' latest navigation improvements on the Ouachita River drowned the shallow, rippling gravel bars under sediment-laden pools. Dad knew the location of these unique habitats even if they were hidden under winter backwater, and the 7½-horsepower Johnson outboard pushed us upstream toward Old Mill, site of a short-lived sawmill, or perhaps toward The Wreck, where the steamboat *Tributary* burned and sank in 1890. Here we anchored, fitted spin-cast rigs with lead weights and 2/0 hooks baited with the crawfish, and flung the offerings into the cold, dark bayou. Almost always we caught the spunky, red-eyed bass.

Many years and a challenging ichthyology class later I learned in no uncertain terms from a favorite professor that smallmouth bass are not native to Louisiana because they are adapted to live in cooler waters. The bass that we caught then on Bayou D'Arbonne are properly called spotted bass, members of the black bass group along with largemouth and true small-mouth bass. Other common names of the spotted bass are Kentucky bass and redeye bass. Resembling slender largemouth bass, spotted bass have black splotches along their sides, and indeed their mouth is smaller than that of their abundant largemouth cousins. We rarely caught a spotted bass of more than two pounds, and the Louisiana state record for the species is less than five pounds.

As Thoreau carried on about the attributes of pickerel in Walden Pond, I preach the endowments of spotted bass. They are still found throughout the state but are much less abundant than they were before most of our rivers and bayous were altered by dams, dredging, and pollution. They tend to be found in areas with more current than those which largemouth bass inhabit and usually choose gravel or rocky areas as spawning sites, habitats that are uncommon in many Louisiana streams. Reeled up from the depths of a mysterious, unseen realm beneath the surface to leap and splash in the still-angled winter sunlight, they seemed to me inspirited treasure with fiery red eyes.

D'Arbonne National Wildlife Refuge was formally created in 1975 when the US Army Corps of Engineers (COE) transferred 17,421 acres to the US Fish and Wildlife Service. COE had purchased the lands and waters (9,535 acres in Union Parish and 7,886 acres in Ouachita Parish) in 93 tracts held by 57 owners at a cost of $2,976,240.54. Five corporations had owned 80 percent of the property, with small parcels held by many individual landowners comprising the balance. The refuge lies along both sides of Bayou D'Arbonne with a northern boundary along the Point/Rocky Branch Road and continuing downstream for fourteen miles to within 1.5 miles of its confluence with the Ouachita River. Most of the area is a deep overflow swamp consisting of bottomland hardwoods with a fringe of uplands on the west and northeast edges. More than half of the refuge experiences backwater flooding from January through May in a normal year, and 87 percent is subject to flooding during atypical events.

As a component of the National Wildlife Refuge System, D'Arbonne NWR inherited broad goals of that unique assemblage of federal lands and waters. These include actions to:

- perpetuate the migratory bird resource,
- preserve a natural diversity and abundance of fauna and flora on refuge lands,
- preserve, restore, and enhance in their natural ecosystems all species of animals and plants that are endangered or threatened with becoming endangered, and
- provide an understanding and appreciation of fish and wildlife ecology and humans' role in their environment and to provide refuge visitors with high-quality, safe, wholesome, and enjoyable recreational experiences oriented toward wildlife, to the extent these activities are compatible with the purposes for which the refuge was established.

In addition to this overall mission, all refuges have individual purposes established by the legislation or executive order that created them. For D'Arbonne NWR the legislative purpose is for the "conservation, maintenance and management of wildlife, resources thereof, and its habitat thereon."

When the refuge was created, the natural resources within its boundaries had long been exploited. Beginning in the early 1900s the mature forest was removed in waves to meet market demands. When the T. L. James Co., one of the largest pre-refuge landowners, got wind of the government's plan to buy their property, they began cutting all merchantable timber. Much of the upland areas had been farmed until abandoned by the late 1950s. Early pine plantations were attempted along Holland's Bluff Road when loblolly and slash pine were planted in 1949–1950. Fusiform rust, a type of fungi, eventually eliminated most of the non-native slash pines. A casual glimpse of an aerial map reveals a large anthropomorphic artifact in the form of a clearing in the middle of the refuge. There, in 1954, a timber company bulldozed a thousand acres in an experiment to farm baldcypress, sweetgum, and water tupelo. Except for a few baldcypress, the plantings did not survive. Following the soybean craze that swept down the Lower Mississippi Valley in 1966, the size of the field was increased by half and planted in the promising new crop from China. This venture failed too after three consecutive years of flooding, the site, after all, being in the middle of a swamp. On the same aerial map a straight line, rare in natural settings, denotes the remains of Bayou Choudrant after it was channelized in 1967 to improve drainage for timber harvests. The new refuge staff thus inherited a greatly disrupted expanse of forested wetlands. As they assessed their new charge, it became obvious that the priority management objective in broad terms would be to help the swamp heal.

I was finishing up graduate school with a degree in Wildlife and Fisheries Science when the refuge was established. Living a state away and many miles from a legitimate swamp, I could imagine no better job than to work on the new national wildlife refuge now overlaying the place where I first slept under the stars while serenaded by barred owls, gathered spring mayhaws for Mother's jelly, shot wood ducks for Thanksgiving dressing, and found the mysterious stone dart points of people long vanished—in essence, the place where I had grown to manhood. I was then (and continue to be) in Aldo Leopold's camp when he said, "There are some who can live without wild things and some who cannot." I did get the job on the refuge as manager-in-charge, but it was many years after I graduated. In the meantime, my return path to the D'Arbonne Swamp meandered through forests and marshes of ten other national wildlife refuges, all harboring spectacular natural resources and wonderful adventures.

A name change may be in store for my favorite understory tree in the D'Arbonne Swamp. Mayhaws are small trees found in forested wetlands of the Southeast that produce a fruit used to make one of the finest jellies ever to grace a buttermilk biscuit. Technically considered hawthorns in the rose family, they grow to thirty feet tall and thrive in overflow swamps with slightly acidic soils and a sandy component. They are thus rare in the heavy clay soils near the Mississippi River and common along the Ouachita/Black River system and its tributaries. D'Arbonne Swamp is ideal mayhaw habitat. In fact, the national champion mayhaw as recognized by American Forests resided on the refuge until a few years ago when it succumbed to old age.

Mayhaws are an important food source for many kinds of wildlife. Deer, raccoons, squirrels, opossums, and several species of birds relish the fruits. Native Americans undoubtedly consumed them for thousands of years, and the first Europeans quickly learned of their value. One pioneer Louisiana diary account reveals that mayhaw gathering could be quite an adventure. Miss Caroline Poole, a schoolteacher in the frontier village of Monroe, writes in her entry of May 7, 1836, "Hunt for May-haws. Rode sixteen miles on horseback. Saw rattlesnake. Crossed bayous where the water was above the saddle skirts, thirty yards wide. Saw black snakes in abundance. Camped in the woods. Coffee. Bacon cooked on a stick. Enjoyed the day but very much fatigued." A note in *The Gazette* of Farmerville on May 2, 1894, reads, "Mayhaws are ripening and the teeth of the small boy will soon ware a wire edge, but he will cut the mayhaws all the same." Currently, during years of abundant crops, hundreds of thousands of pounds of mayhaws are gathered from Louisiana swamps by individual connoisseurs. A commercial market has also been developed, and it's now possible to enjoy a fine local mayhaw wine with the exquisite jelly on that buttermilk biscuit. Even the politicians got involved when in 2014 they designated the mayhaw as the official state fruit tree of Louisiana, and mayhaw jelly as one of the two official state jellies (the other is sugar cane jelly).

The white mayhaw flowers traditionally appear in February and March and often present the first splash of spring color to local swamplands. Flowers usually occur before and during the emergence of leaves. Marble-size reddish fruits resemble small apples and customarily ripen in May and June. An old axiom claims, "If mayhaws flower in the water, they will fall in the water." This refers to the backwater flooding common to most mayhaw habitats. Studies have shown that trees standing in water have a delayed bloom period. In the small mayhaw patch in the Rocky Branch bottom just north of our house, we have gathered the cherished fruits for thirty-five years. Crops have been naturally cyclic in abundance according to rainfall and the prevalence of diseases such as cedar apple rust, which has a life cycle that passes through eastern redcedar trees on its path to infect and deform mayhaw fruits. But there is a new reality in that winters are warmer now on average. Regardless of the presence or absence of backwater, the trees bloom earlier and in turn the fruit ripens earlier, often by as much as a month. I anticipate the jelly from my favorite understory tree will soon be labeled "aprilhaw," a result of very real climate change in the D'Arbonne Swamp.

10

An Ailing Forest—Missing Mussels—Lost Fish

In the early 1990s refuge foresters began to have an uneasy feeling about changes they were seeing in the treetops on some areas of D'Arbonne NWR. They noticed the highest, outermost branches in the crowns of many trees were dying. The anomalies turned out to be harbingers of mortality at a scale never before observed in this region as the dieback moved progressively from outer branches inward and downward to eventually kill most affected trees within one to three years. Early on, an expert in tree pathology from the US Forest Service's Southern Hardwoods Laboratory in Stoneville, Mississippi, was enlisted to assess the situation. He designed and implemented a research project, but it was never completed when he changed jobs. His preliminary findings revealed mortality to be almost totally restricted to willow oaks, most of which were in solid stands fifty to sixty years old. Adjacent overcup oaks were OK. The declining trees often had rotten areas on roots and trunks caused by fungi and bacteria. They were also infested with wood-boring insects. Perhaps most telling, the affected trees were growing only on two soil types that tended to be drought prone when not flooded. Groom soils have a relatively thin (12 to 15 inches) clay-silt layer over silty-sand, whereas Litro soils have a deeper (24 to 36 inches) clay-silt layer over silty-sand. Oak roots tend to be restricted to the clay-silt layer, and mortality was higher on Groom soils.

So what happened here that caused a relatively healthy 2,500-acre forest to up and die at this point in time? For those of us who have prowled about this area for a long while, there was an obvious smoking gun in the shape of the latest downstream dam on the Ouachita River. The US Army Corps of Engineers' new nine-foot channel altered the natural hydrology where the willow oaks lived. The site is much wetter now, especially during the critical, first third of the growing season. Although adapted to flooding during the dormant season and occasional, irregular inundation in the growing season, the trees could not withstand the pressure of such stress on an annual basis. Add to this recipe for disaster the droughty soils, especially Groom soils, which flip the water regime to the other extreme when floodwaters abate, and the diminished ability to resist pathogenic fungi and bacteria. The results should not be surprising.

In an effort to mitigate the calamity, refuge foresters began to cut the dying hardwoods using commercial loggers to remove most of the trees so that sunlight could reach the ground and accelerate the growth of otherwise shade-intolerant seedlings. The hope is that the seedlings will grow into a new forest that is adapted to the new conditions. It's a long shot, as the reality is that all of the stress inducers are still present and trees continue to die.

John Harris lay face down on the bottom of Bayou D'Arbonne in ten feet of water. Visibility in the murky bayou was zero as he groped the mud totally blind to his surroundings. It was the week before Thanksgiving in 2016, and an early frost that tinged the adjacent cypress trees with russet needles chilled the water temperature to an uncomfortable degree even in a wetsuit. Dr. Harris is a malacologist, a person who studies mollusks. His job on this and following days was to survey the mussel fauna of the thirteen-mile section of bayou within the national wildlife refuge. An assistant in the boat above monitored a hookah rig apparatus that provided a steady supply of air down to the diver. Survey protocol was to collect all encountered mussels on transects running perpendicular to the channel. Beginning at the Point/Rocky Branch bridge where the bayou enters the north end of the refuge, transects were established through the refuge at 200- to 500-yard intervals.

Freshwater mussels are a little-known, at least to the general public, but critical component of the biodiversity of many bayous, streams, and rivers. Related to the much-sought-after oysters of coastal areas, freshwa-

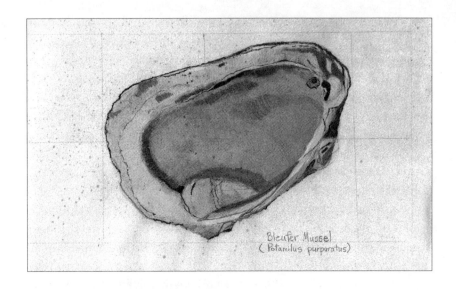

Bleufer Mussel
(Potamilus purpuratus)

ter mussels in Louisiana are not usually consumed by people today. Such was not always the case, however, as Native Americans routinely harvested large volumes of the high protein food. Piles of discarded shells called middens still mark the campsites of prehistoric peoples in this region. Early in the twentieth century, hundreds of button factories along the Mississippi River used freshwater mussel shells to make pearl buttons. Commercial harvesters collected thousands of tons of shells for the factories, which cut, drilled, and polished the pearlescent shell into buttons. A Louisiana Office of Conservation report states "fully 6,000 tons of these shells were taken from our water bodies during the calendar year ending Dec. 31, 1916. Some 4,500 tons of this total were taken from the Ouachita River . . ." Development of the plastics industry sounded the death knell for button factories as inexpensive plastic buttons soon replaced those made from mother-of-pearl. Later in the 1980s, a renewed interest in freshwater mussels occurred when Japanese cultured pearl research revealed that tiny pieces of American mussel shells seeded into oysters made the ideal nuclei around which mother-of-pearl developed.

Ecologically, mussels are critical to many aquatic ecosystems as filters of suspended particles. They feed by siphoning water through hair-like structures called cilia and sorting out plankton and organic materials. Some researchers have found that healthy mussel populations can actually filter the entire volume of a stream in a short period of time. In doing so, they are vulnerable to pollutants from agricultural and industrial runoff. Chemicals, pesticides, and erosional sediments from poor logging and farming practices destroy many mussel beds. Water quality then deteriorates even further when the natural filters are eliminated.

About sixty-five species of mussels inhabit Louisiana waters. Three are considered endangered. Because of their sensitivity to environmental pollution, mussels are referred to as indicator species. When the health of a stream's mussel population declines, it usually means other native plants and animals in the same ecosystem will soon be disrupted—and so it goes right on up the line until humans are the ones impacted.

Dr. Harris returned to the dive boat with three bankclimbers at the first site and only one threeridge at the next downstream location. When completed, his surveys of 37 transects on Bayou D'Arbonne yielded 347 live mussels representing the following twelve species:

Amblema plicata	Threeridge
Cyclonaias pustulosa	Pimpleback
Lampsilis teres	Yellow Sandshell
Leptodea fragilis	Fragile Papershell
Obliquaria reflexa	Threehorn Wartyback
Plectomerus dombeyanus	Bankclimber
Potamilus purpuratus	Bleufer
Pyganodon grandis	Giant Floater
Quadrula quadrula	Mapleleaf
Toxolasma texasiense	Texas Lilliput
Utterbackiana suborbiculata	Flat Floater
Villosa lienosa	Little Spectaclecase

What does this mean? How does one assess the results of the findings? Comparisons to other, similar data are helpful. The only other known list of Bayou D'Arbonne mussels contains twenty-three species and most were collected before 1893. Fourteen of these species were not found in the latest survey. Dr. Harris reasons that the historic Bayou D'Arbonne mussel community would have been similar to that of Bayou Bartholomew, also a

Ouachita River tributary a few miles to the north where thirty-five species have been collected. Although Bayou Bartholomew is much longer, the watersheds are similar in size. It is also free-flowing and has never been channelized. His conclusions are that the impoundment of Bayou D'Arbonne Lake in 1964 and the Ouachita-Black rivers navigation project in 1974 "have likely substantially impacted the mussel fauna within D'Arbonne NWR." The types of mussels found on both sites provide further clues. Most of the species in Bayou D'Arbonne are generalists capable of adapting to lentic (nonflowing) water bodies as opposed to those in Bayou Bartholomew that need a lotic (flowing) water system. It is also worth noting that mussels in Bayou D'Arbonne are heavily skewed to one species, *Plectomerus dombeyanus,* which made up more than 76 percent of all those encountered in the survey. Likewise, the density of mussels in Bayou D'Arbonne was far less than in other regional streams sampled in recent times. In summary, Dr. Harris once again states that the "U.S. Army Corps of Engineers operation and management of Columbia Lock and Dam and operation and management of Lake D'Arbonne by the Bayou D'Arbonne Lake Commission have likely substantially affected the species richness, relative abundance, and distribution of mussels in Bayou D'Arbonne within D'Arbonne NWR."

As plans for construction of Lake D'Arbonne were being finalized, a young graduate student who would later have a long career as a local fisheries biologist, chose as his thesis project to survey the fish fauna of the D'Arbonne and its tributaries before they were impacted by the lake. Bobby Walker set out in 1960 with seines, hoop nets, minnow traps, trotlines, rotenone, slat traps, dip nets, and hook and line. He stated, "The purpose of this study is to supply data which may be compared with similar data collected at a future date in order to evaluate the effects of this impoundment upon the species of fishes now present." Working from nineteen established stations scattered along the bayou and up the tributaries, he collected and identified seventy-nine species of fish. Aquatic habitat at the various stations varied from deep, mud-bottomed channels to shallow riffle areas with sand and gravel substrate. As might be expected, some species were found throughout the drainage system and other, often rare species were restricted to specific habitats. Walker's concluding prediction was, "With all things considered, sports fishes and commercial fishes should flourish, while some of the seemingly less important species will be adversely effected."

Twenty years later, after the Corps of Engineers dam on the Ouachita River and the Lake D'Arbonne project were realities, Mike Wood, another budding fisheries biologist, titled his thesis "A Taxonomic Survey of the Fishes of Bayou D'Arbonne after Impoundment." His sampling protocol was similar. At twenty stations he used the same tools as Walker but added gill and trammel nets, and electrofishing. His more intensive survey yielded eighty-eight species of fish in the same basic area, much of which was now in the depths of Lake D'Arbonne. Wood collected thirteen species in this survey that were not found in pre-impoundment collections, likely a result of more sampling and electrofishing, since most would be expected to be present in the area before the dams. What he did not collect is more telling. Ten species previously reported were not found in his survey. Wood determined,

The fishes of Bayou D'Arbonne can be divided into three groups based on their distribution within the drainage. These groups are fishes inhabiting the smaller tributaries, fishes inhabiting the mainstream and backwaters, and fishes that are found throughout the study area. . . . Swift running streams with rock bottoms and shallow riffle areas with sand and gravel substrates are now hidden under lakes or swollen mainstream areas. Consequently, the fish fauna has changed dramatically. Several [regionally common] species, which were found in small numbers and some which were not collected in the pre-impoundment survey, are now abundant and widely distributed in the system. One example is *Dorosoma petenense,* the threadfin shad, which was found to be rare in the 1965 study with but two specimens reported from one location. In this study, the threadfin shad was found at eight sampling stations and was represented by 6,466 specimens.

But it is the ten species absent from Wood's survey that is troubling, the ones Walker labeled "seemingly less important species." These were uncommon to begin with in their habitat of shallow, riffled waters, unknown to the public with names like steelcolor shiner, speckled darter, and stargazing darter, and Wood says of them, "Most of these species share similar preferences for a now absent habitat."

Detailed research on other local streams verifies the ruinous (in terms of maintaining biodiversity) impacts of tampering with natural aquatic systems. Five streams flow more or less north/south in the fifty-mile stretch between the Ouachita River and the Mississippi River. From east to west they are Tensas River, Bayou Macon, Big Creek, Boeuf River, and Bayou Bartholomew. All except Bayou Bartholomew have been drastically altered by channelization, dredging, straightening, and low-water dams in the name of flood control and irrigation. Bayou Bartholomew remains relatively unaltered except for levees on some portions. Fewer than fifty species of fish combined now live in all four of the altered streams, mostly those kinds that can survive in warm, muddy water with high levels of salinity. In contrast, 103 species of fish have been documented from Bayou Bartholomew. The fish diversity in Bayou D'Arbonne below the dam falls somewhere between the severely altered streams to the east and Bayou Bartholomew, a reflection of the degree of human meddling.

In contemplating the rightness or wrongness of the willow oak die-off, the probable decimation of natural mussel populations, and the loss of fish diversity in the D'Arbonne Swamp as they relate to construction of the Corps of Engineers dam on the Ouachita River and Lake D'Arbonne, it should be remembered that some considered the establishment of D'Arbonne National Wildlife Refuge as mitigation for the detrimental impacts of the navigation project on natural resources. This idea is not found in the legislative documents that created the refuge, but it's nonetheless true that without the COE dam there would be no national wildlife refuge here. So would the D'Arbonne Swamp be better off without the dam and the accompanying refuge? One only has to look at that part of the swamp beyond the refuge boundaries to see harmful resource exploitation with little concern given to fish, wildlife, and natural plant communities. Without the refuge, the area would soon begin to mimic the adjacent, biologically impoverished tree plantations, though not quite to that extent because of the inherent richness of overflow wetlands.

Even with the intact dams it is possible to improve the current conditions in the swamp. As for the mussels, Dr. Harris reports, "If the opportunity presents, reduction of pool level due to Columbia Lock and Dam and allocation of minimum flows from Lake D'Arbonne through designer flow regimes would likely improve habitat conditions for freshwater mussels." The same tack could also benefit rare fish and stressed oaks. It is politics though that bolsters the management of both dams.

11

Cousin Ollice & Springs—Swamp Religion

My first cousin once removed, Ollice knows a lot about flowing springs. She also knows that the patterns on livestock feed sacks were once of considerable importance to local women. Ollice grew up on the edge of the D'Arbonne Swamp during the Depression and lives there now alone except for a mixed pack of Chihuahua dogs and tabby cats. Clutching her walking stick and adjusting her hearing aids to catch my prying questions, she speaks incisively on these subjects and others. When her father, my great-uncle Clarence, bought feed in Farmerville, the women of the household instructed him to make every effort to get sacks with matching patterns. They sewed clothes, especially dresses, from the cotton sacks, and some semblance of fashion was important even during those hard times. Barring matching material, a clash of steam locomotives and rising suns on a girl's shift would require dye from green walnut hulls to temper the disparity of designs. Evidence of the women's work was always on full display on wash day at the spring when after the laborious chore, clothes were hung to dry on lines strung between the tall trees.

Weather permitting, Ollice and other women of her kin by blood and marriage who lived nearby gathered at the spring weekly to thrash the hard labor stains of the fields and kitchens from their simple apparel. Their domestic tools for the task included large, round-bottomed wash pots that held twenty gallons of water. Three short, stubby legs when placed on iron rocks balanced the kettle, and a pair of opposing iron loops on the rim could support the pot if hung by a chain from a tripod. The exterior was always charred sooty black from the fat pine fires that heated the contents. Wash day was an arduous ritual that involved building and maintaining a hot fire under the pots so that clothes could be boiled before undergoing a series of rinses in nearby tin tubs. Accessible, clean water was a necessity as each washing required several pots of heated water. For Ollice the spring was located halfway between her parents' house and the dogtrot homestead of her grandfather Rufus.

Dependable springs were once a treasured resource on any property. They were often the sole source of water for drinking, cooking, washing, and life in general. For many people in the hill parishes, including the area around the D'Arbonne Swamp, shallow hand-dug wells and springs provided water until subsidized community water systems, which rely on deep, bored wells, were developed. Where springs exist, they are conduits in the water cycle. Rainfall seeps underground by percolating through tiny spaces between soil particles and is stored in porous sands or rocks. The exact land surface where water seeps underground and contributes to a specific spring is called that spring's recharge basin. In areas where soils are mostly heavy clays such as the delta parishes, rainfall doesn't soak in as fast, and runoff into lakes, rivers, and other wetlands is a more natural process. For this reason springs are rare east of the Ouachita River, and most early settlers in that region depended on cisterns for a water supply.

Springs were very common in the hill parishes though. William Darby wrote in 1816, "This river [Bayou D'Arbonne] is supplied by a great number of springs; its water is extremely pure." They formed where groundwater was pushed up to the surface as a result of differences in slope in the shallow aquifers. As rain falls and percolates underground, pressure is exerted on water already in the aquifer and forces some out through natural openings. Ollice's spring surfaced on a hillside beneath the roots of a giant white oak. It flowed into a cypress-encased spring box where fresh milk was stored in the cold water and out through an open-ended pipe eventually making its way to the nearby swamp. For years it served the household needs of several families and the boilers of my great-grandfather's small, steam-powered cotton gin and sawmill.

A while back Amy and I purchased the property where the old spring lies. We call it the Spring Place. It and most others in the region are mere remnants of their once-flowing glory. Many have disappeared completely as a result of depleted water tables and developed or otherwise disturbed recharge basins. Shallow aquifers are particularly susceptible to contamination from fertilizers, pesticides, and other pollutants making even the survivors unsafe as drinking water. As for our spring, it was almost certainly impacted by the drilling of shallow natural gas wells, at least two of which are within a hundred yards.

As children, Ollice and her brothers were tasked with the chore of keeping a goggle-eye bream (aka warmouth sunfish) alive and well in the spring box. This involved cane poles, earthworms, and cork bobbers in the bayou down the hill. The transplanted fish's job was to eliminate mosquito larvae and other insects in the clear pool of water. Today we call this approach "biological control." But today the spring dries up in the summer and cannot support fish. Even when it is flowing, it lacks the volume to reach the swamp. Only the half-buried cast-iron fire dogs from the steam engine remain. In her nineties now, Ollice alone sees the patterns on the feed sack dresses hanging from the propped-up clothes lines.

Just a few feet from my parents' graves facing resurrection east in the Rocky Branch Cemetery, I picked up a broken but finely worked piece of Arkansas chert with distinct fluting that dated it to the Paleo period, perhaps ten thousand years ago. The point of an atlatl spear belonging to an Amerindian who lived a hundred centuries ago and who left the object on ground later consecrated by Euro-Americans, it rests in my collection as a reminder of religions that have wafted like incense over the D'Arbonne Swamp.

We cannot know in detail the spiritual beliefs of the first humans in this region but generalities gleaned from artifacts worldwide and historic encounters with their descendants portray lives richly steeped in divine mysticism, lives unthinkable without a realm of omnipresent spirits beneficial and otherwise. One Louisiana anthropologist wrote, "The Louisiana Indians lived in a sacred world. They made no distinction between the sacred and profane, and saw none of the polarities inherent in the European world view. Their universe was a whole held together by spiritual forces that caused man to respect all things, living and nonliving." The profusion of monumental mounds in the Lower Mississippi Valley, including those along Bayou D'Arbonne, are believed by archaeologists to have facilitated religious activities in most instances. We should remember that some, like the earthworks at Poverty Point, required more labor to construct than St. Paul's Cathedral or the Hagia Sophia, all in the name of religion.

Religions evolve no less than flora and fauna. Changes in the social environment as well as the physical serve as catalysts for shifts in orientation. Advances in technology such as corn-based agriculture, dramatic climate change (e.g., long-term droughts), perhaps even a single charismatic leader resulted in spiritual mutations that manifested as native religions during the first European contacts. Some endure today even after four hundred years of cultural assault. Kaitlin Curtice, a citizen of the Potawatomi Nation and Christian author, offers a common thread woven into most surviving Native American religions, "The bloodline of God is connected to everything . . . shells on the ocean shore, the mushrooms growing in the forest, the trees stretching to the clouds, the tiniest speck of snow in the winter, and our dust-to-dustness—we are all connected and tethered to this sacred gift of creation."

Discounting the brief meanderings of Hernando de Soto's expedition in the Lower Mississippi Valley in the 1540s with priests in tow, the ephemeral French-Canadian trappers of the late seventeenth century, and even the later French traders from south Louisiana, all of whom were Catholic if they were anything at all, Native Americans in this area were spared the intrusions of European religions. Here they succumbed to other aggressive stresses inflicted by the newcomers and soon vanished.

When Don Juan Filhiol was sent by Spanish authorities to establish a wilderness settlement on the Ouachita River just downstream from the mouth of Bayou D'Arbonne, he found a local non-Indian population of only 207 in 1785. The commandant discovered his constituents were mostly free-spirited hunters without permanent dwellings and possessing a disdain of authority of any type—not the characters one would choose as model citizens for a productive, civilized settlement. His writings reflect his frustrations with those "living a life of the greatest independence, placing work in horror, knowing hardly if they were Christian." Increasingly frustrated with those he considered immoral heathens, Filhiol tempted them with promises of a church for proper marriages and baptisms, and a schoolmaster to educate their children. There were few takers in the early years.

Dr. R. F. McGuire, a prominent Ouachita Parish physician, planter, and diarist in the first half of the nineteenth century, lived just below the mouth of Bayou D'Arbonne. On November 13, 1833, he recorded a "most singular rain of fire from the Heavens [that] appeared to start from a center almost East at an elevation of about 65 degrees above the Horizon a little South of East and fell in every direction to the Horizon, creating a light like day-break and every few minutes one so large as to produce a glare. Thousands in view at once from 12 oclock until daylight. The most grand display of fireworks ever witnessed." Many people along the rivers and bayous of Louisiana got Hell scared out of them on that early morning. Clergymen reported sudden, widespread confessions followed by conversions of sinners as definitive signs of the Apocalypse engulfed their world. Indeed, every living human east of the Rocky Mountains in North America was exposed to phenomena with heavenly origins never since repeated in history. It is noted in the chronicles of scientists of the day, of Native Americans, and of Deep South slaves. On this date a meteor storm of such intensity as to be nearly unimaginable occurred. We now know that the event was part of the annual Leonid meteor shower that occurs each autumn when Earth passes through the debris field of particles left by the comet Tempel-Tuttle. At the peak of the 1833 incident, reliable sources reported over 200,000 meteors per hour. Night was turned to day. Another Louisiana man wrote, "There came on a complete shower of stars. They fell for two hours from the clouds, as thick and fast as a July shower of rain, and continued until the sun destroyed their light . . . the earth was so illuminated at intervals that a pin could be seen at any moderate distance." Lakota Indians recorded the event on their buffalo skin calendars. Afterward, slaves in different areas of the South reckoned their age from "the year the stars fell." One slave woman remembered,

> Somebody in the quarters started yellin' in the middle of the night
> to come out and to look up at the sky. We went outside and there
> they was a fallin' everywhere! Big stars coming down real close to
> the groun' and just before they hit the ground they would burn up!
> We was all scared. Some o' the folks was screamin' and some was
> prayin'. We all made so much noise, the white folks came out to
> see what was happenin'. They looked up and then they got scared,
> too. But then the white folks started callin' all the slaves together,
> and for no reason, they started tellin' some of the slaves who their
> mothers and fathers was, and who they'd been sold to and where.
> The old folks was so glad to hear where their people went. They

made sure we all knew what happened . . . you see, they thought it was the Judgment Day.

There are no records to determine if the religious convictions were lasting, but history suggests that most were as ephemeral as the meteors.

The religious tide began to turn when the federal government completed surveys of the region, allowing legitimate land claims, and opening it to settlement. Beginning in the late 1830s, thousands of middle-class farmers immigrated to Union Parish from Mississippi, Alabama, Georgia, and Tennessee. Their hump-backed traveling trunks held treasured family Bibles; their hearts and minds harbored the beliefs of devout Protestants. In short order the D'Arbonne Swamp was surrounded by small groups of people gathering to worship in log cabin homes or under brush arbors on hot summer nights when the crops were laid by. They were threatened and encouraged by circuit-riding preachers bent on collecting souls for Heaven, Hell be damned. Soon after, the first church buildings began to appear with names that evoked Old World Christian geography—Antioch, Bethel, Zion Hill, Calvary, Canaan, and Shiloh. Most originated as or evolved to become Baptist denominations, although a few of Methodist, Church of Christ, and Assembly of God faith sprouted in the spiritual wilderness.

In the small community of Rocky Branch, where I live, three active churches address the spiritual needs of maybe three hundred people on a fair-weather Easter morning. The oldest, Pleasant Hill Baptist Church, was established in 1872 as the Baptist Church of Christ at Pleasant Hill by people whose offspring later married into my family. Across the dirt road in 1918, a "bona fide" Church of Christ sprang up, siphoning off members of the first church and igniting a minor ruckus that lasted for decades. Ostensibly about church doctrine, the rift was likely as much about differences in human nature as are common everywhere. Regardless, the Rocky Branch churches and others scattered around the swamp continue to provide vital spiritual nourishment to many.

Organized religion is most powerful for me in its music. The lyrics and rhythms of the old hymns grasp with tribal, even primal, talons my sense of timelessness in the seasons of life. It was the same for my grandmother McDonald, who spent her last years in a Farmerville nursing home just up the hill from Lake D'Arbonne. A church pianist for decades, she continued in her late nineties to play each Sunday morning for the residents. Almost blind, she turned the pages in the navy blue United Methodist Hymnal at the proper time while playing, even though she could not see a single note in the book.

Sounds of religion still permeate the swamp. On a west wind, I can often hear the distant peals of an electronic bell from a church in Point. I once performed a baptism in the swamp as a favor for a beloved local preacher who was physically unable to conduct the ritual. The individual was a down-on-his-luck, terminally ill man, an avoider of churches who had nevertheless decided that maybe now was the time, just in case. Several carloads of us met on the bayou bank at Holland's Bluff on a late summer afternoon. The water was tepid and seasonally stagnant as I waded waist-deep with the silent candidate. The others crowded close on the bank and I said the words, "In obedience to our Lord and Savior Jesus Christ, and upon your profession of faith in Him, I baptize you my new brother in the name of the Father, Son, and Holy Ghost." I tilted him backward into the D'Arbonne and lifted him up. When he broke the surface we were both instantly immersed again, but this time in song. The onlookers in perfect harmony sent three verses of "Amazing Grace" drifting up and down the bayou, through the draping Spanish moss where parula warblers nested, and into the knotholes of the tallest cypress trees. I could imagine that every life form, plant and animal, within a mile was baptized in song along with me. In those moments at least, we were already in Heaven.

When I think back to that human who crafted the atlatl point on ground that became the edge of the swamp, I am convinced that his beliefs were no less valid than mine, perhaps even more so. All of creation is indeed sentient, responsive, and sacred. As Barry Lopez once noted, "A culture like ours, poorly trained in metaphorical expression and presentation, completely misunderstands most traditional stories. We also have a large number of people who are very difficult to communicate with, because they've given themselves over entirely to the rational mind. They are literal to the point of neurosis." It's a timely sermon.

12

"Natural" Gas—Looking but Not Seeing—
Putting a Name on It—Trauma

If all the living organisms in the oceans of the world could be funneled across a hypothetical set of marine scales to be weighed and categorized to determine which species contributed the largest biomass, we would find that the great whales are not even in the running. Nor would be all of the many types of fish combined. Same for all of the shellfish and seaweeds. The winner by a long shot would be a group of tiny, single-celled algae known as diatoms. By combined weight, diatoms comprise almost half of all life in the oceans. Their influence is such that they generate up to half of the oxygen on Earth annually. Even in death they impact the world in countless ways. For example, trillions of them that lived 75 million years ago continue to weigh on the well-being of modern flora and fauna in the D'Arbonne Swamp today.

The expanse of time involved is almost incomprehensible. Consider that the life span of diatoms is about six days, after which like a slow rain their microscopic bodies laden with energy originally obtained from the sun fall to the ocean floor in a nonstop shower that continues for millions of years. Eventually, their silicon-infused carcasses pile up in porous deposits hundreds of feet thick. Sea levels rise and recede as geological processes continue, sometimes burying the diatom deposits (which also contain the remains of other sea life) under thousands of feet of sand, silt, and rock. Subjected to the high pressures and intense heat of the massive overburden, chemical bonds in the diatoms are rearranged, resulting in the formation of

Natural Gas Well

coal, petroleum, or natural gas. This process occurred at many places around the world, including part of what is now the D'Arbonne Swamp. Buried just over two thousand feet below the surface, a layer of chalky sands infused with natural gas rested innocuously for millions of years.

The first commercial release of that natural gas, which can be considered recycled solar energy first stored in the diatoms via photosynthesis, was due in part to a colorful Romanian immigrant to northeastern Louisiana. After a stint in the early Texas oil fields, Louis Lock came to Monroe to promote the idea of drilling a local exploratory well. He found financial backers and more or less arbitrarily picked a site thirteen miles east of the D'Arbonne Swamp. A wooden derrick was soon erected and drilling began in June 1916. After about two weeks the night crew encountered tremendous pressure that almost blew the drill out of the hole. A local publication reported that by the next morning Lock was running through the streets of Monroe, firing a pistol into the air and shouting, "We've got it! We've got it!" in his heavy Romanian accent.

What Lock assumed he had was oil, since in many areas natural gas and petroleum exist in the same formation. After flaring the high-pressure gas to the side for two weeks, drilling resumed until a zone of salt water was penetrated, at which point the well was abandoned. Lock and his investors were disappointed. Natural gas was basically worthless at the time because pipelines did not exist to move the product to markets. Other wells were drilled in the area in the next few years with the same results—abundant natural gas but no oil. Eventually, though, a transportation infrastructure was built to serve what became known as the Monroe Gas Field, one of the largest early gas fields in the United States, encompassing 425 square miles north and west of the town of Monroe.

Over the years economics drove the development of the field and generally limited wells to one per forty acres. Beginning in the 1970s a striking, short-lived spike in natural gas prices kick-started a frenzy of drilling until 1986 when the number of wells in the field more than doubled. Many were drilled at six-hundred-foot intervals across the landscape. That landscape of the gas field encompassed the southeastern portion of the D'Arbonne Swamp, including five thousand acres within the D'Arbonne National Wildlife Refuge. The Corps of Engineers did not acquire mineral rights when the land was purchased, and all subsurface minerals are retained by private interests. The result is that more than two hundred wells have been drilled on what is now the refuge before and since its establishment. Even though the reservoir is now severely depleted of gas, many of the wells are still producing.

It should surprise no one that mineral extraction is often disruptive to the natural environment. Surveying, seismic activities, clearing and construction of access roads, well sites, pipelines, drilling, maintenance of facilities, and saltwater spills take a toll. Within the refuge, several issues have been documented and include disturbance to wildlife and their habitats. When a forest is fragmented into smaller patches by roads, well sites, and pipelines, cowbird parasitism on songbird nests increases as does disruption to endangered species such as the red-cockaded woodpecker. Abandoned equipment and facilities such as open bore holes and improperly covered mud pits often pose hazards to wildlife and humans. Saltwater, a by-product of natural gas production, was once carelessly dumped into the environment, essentially sterilizing large areas of vegetation; remediation is very difficult. Even when it was contained in shallow pits, seasonal flooding released the concentrated brine into the backwater. Until the 1970s, most meters used to measure gas production contained mercury, which was carelessly handled and resulted in significant amounts of mercury in the soil below the meters. Many of the contaminated sites flooded annually, exposing aquatic organisms to the mercury. Samples of fish in Bayou D'Arbonne revealed elevated levels of mercury in some species and resulted in several official advisories to avoid or limit human consumption of those fish. High levels of mercury were also detected in raccoons and great blue herons on the refuge.

It seems probable that such problems exist at all places in the D'Arbonne Swamp where gas wells are found. Without a doubt the situation is better now than in previous years. Saltwater is pumped back into the ground through injection wells and is no longer released indiscriminately, although the threat of spills remains. Mercury has been removed under many of the meter sites. Doubtless also, none of these improvements would have occurred without the dual threats of liability concerns and enforcement actions. Responsible parties did not come forward voluntarily to clean up the swamp simply because it was the right thing to do. For the present flora and fauna, the postmortem impacts of diatoms remain relevant even after 75 million years.

In 1906 John Martin Goyne was awarded a contract with the state of Louisiana to cut a road from Crossroads to West Monroe. It was first called Green-Briar Road and later White's Ferry Road and runs more or less north-south across the southeast corner of the D'Arbonne Swamp. According to the Louisiana Department of Highways, about four thousand vehicles travel this way each day. Like many natural areas, the swamp is largely unknown to most people passing through it, including those who live nearby. Today, maybe two hundred people in the regional metropolitan area of 175,000 have some familiarity with it and the wild flora and fauna. Their knowledge was acquired for the most part while engaged in the consumptive activities of hunting and fishing, pursuits that for those who are receptive can yield a rewarding environmental education. But for the masses, the swamp and other natural areas are mysterious and even frightening places. More than one hundred years ago, John Muir summed up the situation when he declared, "Most people are on the world, not in it[,] [and] have no conscious sympathy or relationship to anything about them."

With so many distractions, how does one become "in" the natural world today, at least to the point of understanding that our well-being is inseparably linked to that of our environment? A first step is to learn what wild plants and animals live in your area. This must go beyond a vague awareness that different types of trees live in a forest and different kinds of fish swim in the bayou. Learning the names of plants and animals is critical to realizing the richness of biodiversity. Aids abound in the form of naturalist programs, field guides, and websites that specialize in regional plants, birds, insects, reptiles, etcetera. It follows that one cannot learn the names of flora and fauna without becoming curious about their habits and behavior. Emerging insights rouse mental questions such as where do the backyard Baltimore orioles go in winter or are the ubiquitous loblolly pine plantations really forests. As knowledge accumulates it becomes more difficult to ignore headlines declaring unprecedented bird declines (almost 3 billion fewer birds in North America than forty-eight years ago; more than one in four have disappeared). It is easier to understand how the collapse of global insect populations as reported in *National Geographic* and elsewhere will affect humans, including those who drive up and down White's Ferry Road.

Boiling rat skulls on a Coleman stove in my soon-to-be wife's bedroom at her parents' house was one of the steps I undertook to learn the names of wild animals. We were in the final semesters of a college program leading to undergraduate degrees in biology. Deeply immersed in a mammalogy course, we were required to compile a collection of small mammal skins and skulls as a learning tool. D'Arbonne Swamp provided the bottomland hardwood habitat occupied by our target rodent species.

Using small snap traps baited with peanut butter and oatmeal, we set our traplines for the night just before dark and returned the following morning hoping for diverse specimens. We were not trying to capture as many individuals as possible but rather to document the presence or absence of various species in a designated area. After the traps humanely dispatched the animals, our scientific work began according to a rigid protocol. Many types of similar small mammals can be separated to species by differences in their teeth and skull measurements. Thus, the skulls required boiling to remove the flesh for accurate assessment. Additional measurements were taken, including total body length, tail length, ear length, and hind foot length. Each animal was skinned in a prescribed manner; the hide was preserved with 20 Mule Team Borax and stuffed with cotton. After a drying process, we submitted our specimens to the presiding professor for inclusion in the natural history museum. Well-prepared specimens with accurate data enhanced one's chance of an "A" in the course.

The exercise revealed new names to me. The group of animals that I once generically thought of as "rats" became amazingly diverse. Among others, the swamp harbors deer mice (*Peromyscus maniculatus*), woodland voles (*Microtus pinetorum*), eastern wood rats (*Neotoma floridana*), and short-tailed shrews (*Blarina carolinensis*)—these last not even rodents but rather tiny insectivores. Along with new names came new ecological insights. It's amazing how many small mammals are out there! This—in spite of how few I have encountered in all my years in the swamp. Moreover, those species are highly adaptable—able to maintain their populations in an area that floods seasonally to twenty feet. Even so, different species have different habitat preferences. Wood rats prefer areas with vines to climb, while voles like higher ground, such as the embankments of the Cross Bayou Bridge on White's Ferry Road.

Our biology curriculum exposed us to a broad array of animals and plants. In addition to mammalogy, we reveled in herpetology (reptiles and amphibians), ornithology (birds), ichthyology (fish), dendrology (trees), and general plant taxonomy. Other options were available such as entomology (insects), parasitology (parasites), and bryology (mosses and liverworts). Some required collections, some did not, but all entailed learning names of wild flora and fauna including the Latin scientific names in most cases. Scientific names are very helpful when studying similar species but not a necessity for general nature enthusiasts. Learning common names will open the door that gets you "in" the world. Once "in," it's only a small step to comprehend another John Muir verity: "When we try to pick out anything by itself, we find it hitched to everything else in the universe."

I experienced trauma one morning in the late 1970s when I returned to our family camp for the first time in several months. Timber-company lands, where some trees were harvested at infrequent intervals, surrounded our eighty-acre parcel. The neighboring forest was vibrant with a variety of hardwood trees and pines with their attendant understory plants and an assortment of animals that thrived there. But on that morning while driving into the camp, I came upon a scene that my brain, combing all its previous experiences, could not interpret. The forest was literally gone. In its place was a panorama that struck me as identical to those in old black and white photos of Civil War battlefields. Except for a few saplings, leaning and arched like drawn longbows, there were no trees at all, no verticality all the way to the horizon. I was shell-shocked. In the years since that day and on many similar ones, I have viewed the attendant trauma in an evolving series of perspectives—emotional, ecological, and finally spiritual.

Beginning in the 1970s, a calamity of historic proportions for native plants rolled over the higher elevations of the D'Arbonne watershed in the form of intensely managed, industrial tree farms. At that time almost half a million acres of forest existed in Union Parish. More than half was categorized as mixed hardwood/pine. The balance was bottomland hardwoods and upland stands that had already been converted to pure pine. Historically, most of the upland forests were in the mixed hardwood/pine group.

Whereas natural upland forests in this area once consisted of more than a hundred species of native trees and shrubs, tree farms are managed for the production of one species only—artificially grown loblolly pine. All others are discouraged by drastic means. For industrial tree farmers, a scorched earth, clear-cut seedling bed is the most desirable first step. The landscape is "burned down" with herbicides to quash competition from other plants before nursery grown seedlings are planted in straight rows on a six-foot by six-foot grid. The tree farmers usually thin the plantation when the crop is twelve to fifteen years of age, then clear-cut the remaining trees at twenty-five to start the process again. The sole objective of the corporate landowners is to produce the greatest amount of wood fiber in the shortest amount of time. They have been tremendously successful in meeting these goals, so far.

After several decades of industrial tree farming (the third clear-cut of lands around the family camp occurred in 2021), the sight of barren hillsides is commonplace on forest lands throughout the Southeast. In the D'Arbonne watershed, huge expanses of unprotected, red clay soils are now an ordinary sight. Ordinary, but not natural. The color of bare soil varies, and that variation is related to soil fertility. We call dark, rich, organic soils topsoil. Scientists label this layer the "A-horizon." It is a soil full of living microorganisms and decaying plant roots; it stores carbon that would otherwise be released into the atmosphere; and until recently it was common in the pre-clear-cut forests. With the repeated loss of protective plant cover, however, topsoil soon erodes away. Local people figured this out on their own in the years before World War II, as second- and third-generation farmers were forced to move to town when their small patches would no longer support nutrient-sapping cotton. If they don't already know it, the industrial tree farmers will soon learn the same lesson, will soon learn that their intense, short crop rotation is not sustainable in the long run. The entirety of their crop, millions of trees, is derived solely from the sun and now scarce soil nutrients. New harvesting methods like whole-tree chipping return nothing to the site, not even limbs or treetops as in traditional logging practices. Already tree farmers are being forced to bomb their plantations with profit-reducing, nitrogen-based synthetic fertilizers.

The botany of a forest is more than woody plants. In a temperate forest (and one fast becoming subtropical because of global climate change) such as that at Heartwood, hundreds of species of herbaceous plants, wildflowers, grasses, sedges, mosses, and fungi anchor themselves in compatible niches that aggregate into a lush botanical fabric. Animal diversity follows plant diversity, so the faunal wealth of Heartwood is abundant. Tree farms, in contrast, represent a biological desert. Today, three-toed box turtles that forage on our bolete mushrooms are scarce there, and the wood thrush whose spring song inspirits our lives could never survive in the pine monoculture. At my home on Heartwood, wood ducks nest in the hollow cavities of old trees; but on industrial tree farms, any such structure that stands in the way of a pine tree is unwelcome and will quickly be razed. As I write these words, seven deer are foraging white oak acorns just beyond my window. Deer in the pineries survive on invasive Japanese honeysuckle and piles of corn dumped by hopeful hunters. And so it goes for the likes of buttermilk snakes, chinquapins, monarch butterflies, wild turkeys, twayblade orchids, gray fox, etcetera. A natural forest is species rich and in turn enriches the human species. Tree farms as they exist in the D'Arbonne watershed are species-poor, impoverishing those of us who can't see the forest for the trees.

13

An Imaginary Census—Hound Dog Lessons—Truck Terror

Awareness and insight often surface from the depths of imagination. Consider this fanciful exercise as a technique to ponder the natural history of mammals in a southern swamp: Using the D'Arbonne Swamp as the study area, I'll build an elevator-equipped observation tower five hundred feet tall just on the west side of Wolf Brake (heaven forbid anything remotely similar ever actually happening in this beautiful area). Now you can choose the methodology to accomplish the next stage of the tale. Somehow you figure out how to outfit every mammal in the swamp with small, high-intensity LED lights with photocells that activate at dusk. And each species emits a slightly different colored light for identification. After an exhilarating ride to the top of the tower we can behold most of the swamp from the perspective of a soaring red-shouldered hawk. What might we expect to observe in this conceptual game?

White-footed Mouse
(*Peromyscus leucopus*)

Let's go up with a thermos of black coffee and fried apple pies wrapped in wax paper just before sunset on a cool, clear evening in late autumn after most of the leaves have fallen. As the lumens decrease, pinpricks of light emerge from the shadows below, faintly at first, then brighter to the degree that IDs can be determined with the aid of our reference chart. Some lights are moving, some are stationary; some are in clusters, others like a lone match flickering in the darkness. We record it all. Let's do this all night, every night for two weeks, analyze our observations, overlay them on habitat maps, and make some statements about mammals in this swamp at this point it time.

- In general, most of the animals are crepuscular, meaning that they are most active in the twilight hours of dusk and dawn.
- We know that more than forty kinds of mammals live in the swamp, but we did not observe the lights of some. Perhaps a few species of bats had migrated, and the moles were tucked in their underground burrows.
- Rodents are the most abundant mammals in the swamp and include many thousands of white-footed mice, golden mice, fulvous harvest mice, eastern wood rats, cotton rats, and voles. They occupy habitats from the leaf litter to tree canopies. (Rodents comprise about 40 percent of the 2,200+ mammal species on Earth.)
- All of the predators in the swamp eat rodents! The lights have revealed that foraging behavior of foxes, coyotes, mink, and bobcats often result in an extinguished rodent light.
- The animals are never far from food sources unless they are searching for new sources. Raccoons concentrate on ripe persimmons until they are gone and then move on. Ground-truthing a cluster of deer lights in the same place for several nights have revealed a dozen Nuttall oaks on a ridge dropping their copious acorn crop.
- In addition to food sources, breeding behavior affects movements at times. Male white-tailed deer moved several miles in and out of the swamp during the rut. Their travels are usually into the prevailing wind.
- Bayou D'Arbonne does not hinder the movements of most resident mammals, as their lights routinely cross back and forth across the meandering channel.
- We have seen more mammals by species and number on the edges of the swamp where there is a greater diversity of habitats

- (i.e., food and shelter) and easy access to upland refuge during periods of natural flooding.
- Lights/mammals are relatively scarce in some areas of the swamp, usually those low, interior regions subject to deep overflow and with little ground cover.
- Similar species often prefer different habitats. Fox squirrels like open forest with sparse ground cover whereas gray squirrels occupy dense forest with thickets and vines. Swamp rabbits are found throughout the swamp, but cottontails, being averse to swimming, prefer the edges.
- Some mammals have specialized niches, like beavers and their wetlands. Some are highly specialized, like the uncommon Rafinesque's big-eared bats that seek out brakes with large, hollow, water tupelo trees for dens.
- The highway on the east side of the swamp (White's Ferry Road) is a common cause of mortality for deer, raccoons, armadillos, and opossums. Again the lights tell the tale.
- The digestive system of human mammals isn't designed for a prolonged diet of fried apple pies.

This imaginary exercise is an effort to help visualize what goes on in a southern swamp from a natural history perspective. The "statements" are based in reality. Seen through a windshield from the periphery, forested wetlands appear to many people inhospitable and lifeless, void of value. Actually, they are diverse and vibrant with life forms far beyond the mammals considered in this essay. Into the mammalian stew of D'Arbonne Swamp, throw in 200+ species of birds; then add more than sixty types of herps (reptiles and amphibians), followed by all the variety of fish life, and spice with an uncountable number of insects, arachnids, and their kin. All of these dynamic layers are teeming on the landscape with the purposeful intent of maintaining the presence of their species in the long term. It is almost beyond imagination.

One of the joys and hazards of reading is that it can send one down previously unconsidered paths. My favorite childhood book was Wilson Rawls's

Where the Red Fern Grows. Set in the Ozark Mountains, it is a coming-of-age tale about a boy and his two redbone coon hounds and their pursuit of one of the wiliest creatures in the forest. Rife with danger, adventure, sorrow, and joy all played out by a boy my age and his dogs—how much better could a book be? That it was also a fount of life's lessons was not apparent to me at the time.

So after reading this book I was determined to procure my own coon hounds and begin my own adventures in the D'Arbonne Swamp just down the red clay hill from my house. After more than a half century I don't remember how I came up with the money for such expensive dogs but I think it involved a line of credit with my parents and assurances that proceeds from the bountiful 'coon pelts that I would harvest would easily repay my debts. In retrospect, that was an early chapter in one of my own life lessons.

My research into the various breeds of hounds was intense and exhaustive. I read everything I could find about redbones, black and tans, plotts, blueticks, and treeing walkers. Of course, once I selected a breed, I had to find a place to buy one out of good hunting stock. You just couldn't go down to the local pet store and purchase a redbone puppy from proven lineage. I found my source in the classified pages of an *Outdoor Life* magazine—a kennel in Henrietta, Texas, with a brochure full of impressive photos of hounds in full cry as they reared up on big trees bellowing at an unseen quarry. There was also a picture of an old barn whose side was entirely covered with the square-stretched hides of raccoons. That sealed the deal for me.

I ordered two male puppies, a bluetick and a black and tan for $35 each, easily the most expensive purchase in my life at the time. They were to be shipped via air freight to the Monroe airport. Perhaps you can imagine the agony I suffered waiting for their arrival. When the call finally came that they would come in on the next day's flight, I was ready with a newly constructed pen and a doghouse filled with fresh pine straw for the cuddly pups' delight. Mom took me to the airport in our Pontiac station wagon, and I marched straight to the freight desk to claim my puppies. The agent led them out to me. Note that he did not carry them out—he led them out on a leash of doubled-up hay strings. They were seven months old and weighed sixty pounds each. I was still in shock when he handed me the freight bill that was more than the cost of the dogs. Laden with pent-up energy, the hellions promptly dragged me through the lobby and out into the parking lot.

My coon-hound adventures in the D'Arbonne Swamp began the very next night. Adventures, as it turned out, that were considerably less dramatic than those in my favorite book. For the local raccoon population they were the source of occasional benign annoyances with no long-term impacts. There were, however, many exciting episodes involving long nights wandering in the swamp trying to keep up with the hounds, interactions with nontarget species (e.g., skunks and coyotes), and even an offer to trade the bluetick for $100 and ten beagles by an impressed hunter on the west side of the bayou. The story ends sadly for the black and tan, as he contracted distemper that caused him to become cross-eyed and severely bowlegged. He had to be euthanized. The bluetick, however, lived a full life after a coming-out event during which he revealed that he was really a deer hound and not a coon hound.

After a first life in the Mississippi delta somewhere near Clarksdale, and following a modest reincarnation, a 1949 Willys Jeep truck came into my possession. I imagined that it had once been the workhorse used to transport men and supplies to a classic, old-time deer hunting camp or perhaps even to one of the storied duck blinds frequented by Nash Buckingham himself. When my father purchased the pickup for $150, it came with clumps of Sharkey clay still glued tight to the undercarriage. Dad added a rebuilt four-cylinder motor and a pipe bumper and presented it to me as my first motorized means of transportation. I was sixteen years old, two years younger than the truck. It came with one condition—that when I reached the end of our driveway, the truck was only to turn right on the road, never left except to get gas. Left was the way to town, pool halls, bars, and trouble. A right turn led directly to the D'Arbonne Swamp.

My world expanded instantly. Heretofore I was generally limited by how far I could paddle an aluminum boat to run a trotline or how far I could hike to check a trapline after school and yet return home by soon after nightfall. That distance was about a mile each way if by cypress paddle and three miles if by hip boot. The Jeep increased my home range exponentially, and I wasted no time in surveying the boundaries of my new territory. First though, I needed to address the undesirable color of the truck. It was a dingy gray, like damp campfire ashes, a condition that I remedied with a gallon of forest green paint and a four-inch paintbrush from the hardware store in town.

White's Ferry Road was the "highway" in front of our house. It crosses Bayou D'Arbonne a half-mile north on a new bridge that replaced the old ferry and enters the swamp at that point. For five miles the road is elevated fifteen feet above the surrounding wetlands on a berm of soil excavated from a dozen adjacent borrow pits. It is a dependable thoroughfare nowadays except when hundred-year floods refuse to play by the rules. The road shoulders are so steep that there are only a few safe places to get down into the swamp. Those places have earthen ramps and names—"the bridge," "Mose Bayles' Field," "Cross Bayou," and "Dog Pen." In those days they led into the swamp and a maze of logging trails without ends. Timber companies were absentee owners of most of the swamp, and access was unrestricted and free to anyone. Most of the mileage on the odometer of the green Jeep accumulated here.

For a teenage boy the swamp was a teacher of many and diverse lessons. I soon learned of her unforgiving nature as it pertains to the elementary rules of ingress and egress of heavy vehicles on hydric soils. Even the four-wheel-drive Jeep was subject to suddenly squatting in the deep ruts of a wallowed-out mud hole, tires spinning geysers of swamp water fore and aft, requiring a hike of several miles back home. The learning curve was long and often tortuous but not without progress. A low-gear, high rpm, running start became the best method to avoid high-centering in the deep holes. Even then the threat of the large splash drowning out the engine, perhaps even cracking the distributor cap, was real. I learned that a come-along, a type of manual, finger-pinching winch, and log chains were tool kit necessities, along with jumper cables, shovel, and a five-gallon can of extra gas. A pair of vehicles roaming the swamp together was additional insurance.

October 1967 began my first mechanized hunting season. My boyhood friend, Criswell White, and I looked forward to 'coon hunting, our newly acquired interest and one that I credited/blamed on Wilson Rawls because of his novel. We had young hounds that we were sure would soon become champion field trial dogs with our erudite guidance in the D'Arbonne Swamp's abundant raccoon habitat. We planned to hunt together but travel in separate vehicles "just in case." Criswell had to beg to borrow his father's prized 1953 GMC pickup, black in color. Permission was eventually granted, but it came with the unspoken warning of unspeakable doom if it was marred in the slightest fashion. Still, we proceeded with gleeful anticipation.

That October was typically dry until the week before our inaugural hunt when several hours of rain from a tropical depression out of the Gulf of Mexico drenched the thirsty swamp, filling the mud wallows—not a major impediment we reasoned, nothing comparable to that caused by winter rains that last for days. Raccoons being crepuscular mammals, there was no reason for us to head out on that cool Saturday evening until a couple of hours after sunset. This would give the furbearers a chance to prowl about and increase the odds of our hounds striking their trails still hot with scent. About 9:00 p.m. I turned off White's Ferry Road at Cross Bayou with Criswell close behind. We drove down a logging trail through an overcup oak flat and cast the dogs in the direction of Wolf Brake. In no time at all, the black and tan bawled in the distance and was soon joined by the chop-mouthed bluetick. They headed west toward the cypress-tupelo gum brake. Following the maze of logging trails and small pipelines, we bounced the trucks over logs and through potholes in an effort to catch up with the hounds. My excitement led to carelessness and I blundered into a deep mud hole camouflaged in tall grass that captured the Jeep as sure as a steel trap. Luckily, Criswell was able to pull the Jeep backward out of the quagmire. We managed to go around the mud hole, and continued in the direction of the baying dogs. Suddenly, a rain shower passed over, loitering just long enough to grease the swamp's heavy clay soil. The GMC's slick tires lost both traction and steering, and Criswell slid into ruts until I was able to drag him out with the Jeep. Our rescue strategy seemed to be working so far, but then a second shower arrived and lingered. Soon afterward, the dogs showed up. No raccoon, but they seemed proud of whatever it was they had accomplished. We loaded them into the trucks and headed toward

the asphalt road somewhere to the east. In short order Criswell was stuck fast again. This time even the lug tires on the Jeep could not maintain purchase in the rain. When the cable on the come-along broke and our lantern batteries grew dim, we realized the only option was to abandon the GMC until it could be retrieved the following day. On the slippery ride out, with the single wiper blade struggling to clear half the muddy windshield, I could only imagine Criswell's terror at arriving home without his father's truck.

Mr. Julius was known to have a hair-trigger temper that he seemed to reserve for discipline matters regarding his teenage son. Criswell did not reveal the details resulting from his confession other than it involved the "tanning" of "hide." I picked him up after church the next afternoon, and with the repaired come-along we headed back to the swamp to put the whole matter to rest. Having climbed up to the road at the Dog Pen ramp the previous night, the plan was to backtrack from there to the GMC. It didn't happen. Rain had obliterated our tracks, the logging trails seemed to fork in the wrong direction, and our optimism cratered when after several hours of searching with darkness upon us, we grasped that we had lost Criswell's father's truck. I dropped him off two hundred yards from his house in a fog of dread.

The next day after school we resumed the search and rescue operation. Criswell didn't say much; he didn't have to. His dad had to catch a ride to work his graveyard shift at the paper mill. We found the truck within an hour, more or less stumbled upon it, and extracted it with the come-along. It was in the middle of a trail that we had thoroughly searched the previous day as evidenced by the Jeep tracks nearby. Maybe we had just driven past it blinded by the tunnel vision of worry, or not. For the rest of that fall and winter, the green Jeep roamed the swamp alone.

14

A Host of Furbearers Then and Now—Bears Are Back

Raccoons are one of twelve species of mammals considered furbearers by the Louisiana Department of Wildlife and Fisheries. Others include beaver, bobcat, coyote, gray fox, red fox, mink, muskrat, nutria, opossum, river otter, and striped skunk. All twelve reside in the D'Arbonne Swamp. The term "furbearer" is typically used to denote those species that have traditionally been trapped or hunted for their fur and includes both carnivores and rodents. Most have two layers of fur, consisting of a thick, soft underlayer for insulation and waterproofing, and a longer coat of guard hairs for protection. The underlayer is most dense in winter when the pelts are considered "prime" and sought by the fur industry for garments. Trapping seasons are formulated to allow harvest at that time (November 20 through March 31 in Louisiana).

Wildlife managers generally consider fur a renewable resource in that with appropriate regulation populations can be harvested and yet remain relatively stable. In reality, the fickle markets for fur drive the number of animals trapped on an annual basis. Low prices eliminate opportunities for trappers to make a profit. Once a reliable source of supplemental income for some people, trapping in and around the D'Arbonne Swamp has all but ceased.

A few old-time trappers have left us their stories. Thad Johnson lived in the Weldon community and was a part-time trapper along Corney Creek. His diary reveals that in the last two and a half months of 1908 he trapped 54 raccoons, 63 squirrels, 27 mink, 13 rabbits, 7 opossums, 3 ducks, 2 hawks, a cat, and a "big crane." Nicky Haye of Rocky Branch tells of one winter when he was a boy in the early 1940s, during which his dad was sharecropping east of the swamp in the Wall Lake area. He characterizes his family's economic status then as "dirt poor." Just before Christmas his dad set out traps along the river and caught a large male mink. At Bayle's ("We Buy Furs & Pecans") in West Monroe he sold the pelt for $20, the equivalent of a month's income for the family. Nicky said the mink made for a joyous Christmas in their household. Thurston Stokes, a local farmer and trapper, is said to have caught enough mink from the river bottoms in 1912 to pay for forty acres of land. In contrast, a large wild mink pelt today can be expected to bring $8, barely an hour's pay at minimum wage. No one has requested a trapping permit on D'Arbonne NWR in recent years.

Mink are semi-aquatic predators in the weasel family. Nocturnal in habits, they are never far from water. Their diet consists of fish, crawfish, and frogs as well as occasional birds, rats, and mice. They are known to kill much larger swamp rabbits even though the bigger male minks weigh less than three pounds. Once a preferred target of trappers when prices were high, the species should be valued today as an important cog in the swamp ecosystem.

While deer hunting many years ago in the Tensas Swamp near a small brake wonderfully named Bear Wallow, I heard a perplexing clatter coming from the flooded timber. The noise was so puzzling and out of place in this remote area that I determined to seek out its origin. It was a river otter! He was cracking the hard shells of mussels by pounding one atop another on a floating log to get at the tender meat inside. It was one of those magical occasions in the natural world that I'll not likely ever experience again. River otters are cousins of mink, but much larger and even more aquatic. Adult males can weigh more than thirty pounds. Webbed feet, long rudder-like tails, and nostrils and ears that close underwater are adaptations for an aquatic life. Their diets are mostly fish but include mollusks, crawfish, and turtles. Their large, luxurious pelts once brought high prices—which, combined with the relative ease of trapping them, caused inland otter populations to plummet in Louisiana by the 1950s. The loss and contamination of their riverine habitat contributed to their decline. For years otter sightings in the D'Arbonne Swamp were rare. Today, Louisiana hosts a growing yet vulnerable population—an example of the recovery potential of many species when given a bit of protection and an intact environment.

The ubiquitous tracks of raccoons are strewn throughout the swamp as though they fell from a cloud full of paw prints. In their hump-backed, wandering manner, masked like bandits, raccoons forage across the nocturnal landscape as omnivorous generalists feeding on a wide variety of seasonally available foods from crawfish to persimmons. Almost as arboreal as fox squirrels, they prefer hollow trees for denning sites. Speeding vehicles on White's Ferry Road take a toll on them, especially during periods of high water when the highway shoulders offer the only exposed land in the swamp. A good definition of any southern swamp should include the word "raccoon."

Bobcats, foxes, and coyotes represent furbearing predators in the swamp. Their lives are meshed with annual floodwaters when they are driven to adjacent uplands until the waters recede. All feed on a wide variety of small mammals and birds. The foxes and coyotes also eat many wild fruits in season. Coyotes occasionally kill fawns but do not significantly impact deer populations as many hunters claim. Coyotes are recent, highly adaptive members of the swamp fauna, having filled the niche occupied by red wolves since the latter's extirpation. The smaller gray fox is more abundant in the D'Arbonne Swamp than the red fox, which tends to prefer open edges and higher ground. Fox-hunting with hounds in and around the swamp was once a popular activity, providing at times sport and an outdoor venue for men to drink whiskey. Bobcats are common though infrequently observed due to their stealthy, nocturnal habits. Rabbits are a mainstay of their diet, and like many predators bobcats are speciously blamed by hunters for limiting game populations. The following, real, social media post by a local hunter reflects a common sentiment and lack of knowledge concerning predator/prey relationships: "It's totally out of balance. I saw five different bobcats out of my deer stand in the daytime year before last. I heard seven different packs of coyotes, one evening at dark down there. Coons are everywhere. I hunt a lot and am in the woods all during the year. We need year-round trapping!" The attitude toward predators by this hunter and all too many like him can be restated as thus: "If there is the slightest chance that a bobcat (or coyote or bear or any other predator) seen from my deer stand can kill a fawn that could potentially grow up to be a trophy buck that I could potentially shoot, mount, and hang on the wall of my den, then that predator doesn't need to exist." For wildlife biologists, the facts are a hard sell.

As a boy I never heard the startling tail slap of an alarmed beaver in the D'Arbonne Swamp. By 1900 trappers had eliminated them from the state except in a few southern parishes east of the Mississippi River. From those remnant populations in the 1930s beavers were successfully reintroduced throughout the state, their pelts no longer worth enough to incentivize trappers. The first beaver I saw was around 1964 when I was surprised to find one grazing on crimson clover on the earthen approach to the White's Ferry Bridge. Within fifteen years they were common in the D'Arbonne Swamp. Beaver behavior in southern swamps is unlike that of their northern cousins. Flat terrain precludes the need for long, high dams, particularly in those areas subject to annual, natural flooding. During dry periods, small dams across sloughs and creeks suffice to provide adequate habitat. Because water levels in the D'Arbonne Swamp fluctuate as much as twenty feet, stationary beaver lodges that provide shelter and birthing sites are not feasible. Instead they ingeniously build their stick lodges on large, downed logs that float up and down as the water rises and falls. In low-water periods stick lodges are abandoned for dens excavated in banks with submarine entrances. Beavers provide critical wetland habitat for many species, habitat especially important in the D'Arbonne Swamp during long, hot summers. A roll call of wading birds, nesting prothonotary warblers, wood duck broods, fishing raccoons, and otters benefits from beaver-created habitat. The conundrum of their behavior is that permanently impounded trees in beaver ponds die and habitat quality degrades for these species over time. Historically, beavers were abundant in the Lower Mississippi Valley before massive land-clearing and drainage projects reduced the forest size 75 percent from more than 25 million acres to 6.5 million. At the scale of the original forest, beaver "damage" was negligible from an ecological perspective. Today with swamp forests in the region much smaller, the percentage of the total remaining forest impacted by beavers is much greater, thus land managers, even those with strict conservation objectives, often find it necessary to control beaver populations. Such is the case on D'Arbonne NWR, where the aim is not to eliminate beavers but rather to limit the degree of tree mortality from their activities. Refuge foresters identify problem areas where beavers are then trapped and dams removed. As government plans for control activities are properly subject to public review, the ignorance of basic biological concepts by many well-intentioned people are often revealed in their formal comments. A well-known animal rights group in New York once demanded that I, as manager of the refuge, wrap all of the affected trees in metal sheaths to protect them from beavers in lieu of using lethal means. This of course would have entailed encasing several million trees from ground level up to a height of twenty feet. So much for forest aesthetics!

Like beaver, muskrats and nutria are rodents. Once a mainstay of the Louisiana fur industry, muskrats thrived in the brackish coastal marshes but were found only occasionally further inland and almost never in the north half of the state. By the 1970s, apparently in response to a developing rice culture, muskrats appeared in northeast parishes with infrequent sightings along rivers and streams elsewhere in this region. Always rare in the D'Arbonne Swamp, the few sightings are likely transients. Nutrias are natives of South America that were brought to Louisiana before 1930. A number of accounts exist regarding their origins here including intentional releases at various places and escapes of captive animals during hurricanes. Regardless, they found the new environment to their liking, reproduced prolifically as most rodents tend to do, and soon occupied wetlands throughout the state. Their populations were somewhat controlled by trappers as long as fur prices held up but soon exploded in coastal marshes when prices fell. Today in that region a bounty exists on nutria because they literally eat into oblivion coastal wetlands that are additionally suffering from a host of anthropomorphic ailments. Nutria are common but not abundant in the D'Arbonne Swamp, perhaps because deep flooding often restricts access to favored food sources. I see them occasionally in cypress/tupelo brakes and borrow pits. Impacts of this invasive species in this swamp seem to be innocuous.

The Virginia opossum, aka "possum" to most people, wandered in from the waning Cretaceous 65 million years ago and is the only native marsupial in North America. The young are born very premature and spend two months or more in their mother's pouch. Mating does not, as many yet believe, take place through the nose, a belief that likely originated when it was noted that males have forked penises (allegedly to facilitate fertilization in paired nostrils of females). They are common in the D'Arbonne Swamp, especially on the periphery and along streams. Striped skunks are occasionally detected without being observed. Le Page du Pratz wrote in 1758 that the early French settlers of Louisiana called them *bete puante,* or "stinking beast." Uncommon in the swamp proper, they prefer edge habitat near uplands where they can easily seek refuge from high water.

Within the swamp today, furbearer populations are cyclic and fluctuate according to natural ecological restraints. Numbers increase when food, whether plant materials or animal prey, is abundant and decline when times are lean. The size of the annual acorn crop impacts many birds and animals, including raccoons. All are affected by the extent and duration of natural flooding. Long periods of backwater in the swamp reduce rabbit populations, which in turn impacts the reproductive success of their bobcat, fox, and coyote predators. But lengthy backwaters enhance fish populations, which benefit river otters. Diseases in wild animals are often density dependent, meaning large populations are more subject to deadly outbreaks. In this manner distemper can regulate raccoon and mink numbers, and mange afflicts foxes and coyotes. We're now only just beginning to understand these intricate connections and relationships.

A couple of years ago while driving through the D'Arbonne Swamp north of West Monroe, I was treated with a stunning sight. I caught a glimpse of a large animal ahead on the road shoulder, and my first impression was that it must be a hog. As I got closer it became obvious that it was a bear—shiny black and beautiful in the early morning light. He wheeled and ran down the road bank, across a shallow ditch, and into the D'Arbonne National Wildlife Refuge. Several months ago I saw a second one lumbering across Holland's Bluff Road. After a lifetime of prowling about in this swamp, these are my only observations here of the charismatic mammal. Until recent years these encounters would have been nigh on impossible. The Louisiana black bear, the subspecies found in our state and historically occurring throughout Louisiana, had long been eradicated in most of its range. Once sought as a valuable commodity by French-Canadian trappers for their hides and fat, bears were later persecuted as nuisances by white settlers at every opportunity. By the time of President Teddy Roosevelt's famous 1907 bear hunt in Madison Parish, they were restricted in the state to remote areas of the Tensas and Atchafalaya Swamps. Their numbers continued to decline as a result of land-clearing and illegal shooting, and by the mid-1980s when I was a manager of the Tensas River National Wildlife Refuge, our research indicated that they were uncommon even there. Concern by a broad coalition of people across the state resulted in the Louisiana black bear being formally listed under the federal Endangered Species Act in 1992. At the time the population estimate was no more than 150 bears in the state. Since then, work to restore the animals has resulted in another success story for the Endangered Species Act. The current population is estimated at 500 to 750 bears, and it was recently considered recovered and delisted—that is, removed from the Endangered Species list. This is good news for Louisiana, since an important part of our biological and cultural heritage has been saved. It's also good news for the country—another success story for the often-maligned Endangered Species Act. To date this forty-year-old legislation has saved 99 percent of the listed species from the brink of extinction, including our national emblem, the bald eagle; the Louisiana state bird, the brown pelican; and even the icon of our swamplands, the American alligator. Would we be the same without them?

15

Bald Eagle Resurrection—The Value of a Kinglet—Predators
Then and Now—Beguiling Gators—D'Arbonne RCWs on the Edge

What does it say about a country that shoots and poisons its national emblem into extinction? This scenario almost played out in America, at least in the lower forty-eight states. The bald eagle, that majestic raptor that adorns our currency and stands as a symbol of strength and freedom, came perilously close to disappearing throughout its range except in Alaska. The decline began a hundred years ago with human attitudes that considered all predators, including birds of prey, as vermin and targets of eradication at every opportunity. Bald eagles were randomly shot until the first relevant federal law was passed in 1940. Soon after World War II, a new and devastating threat emerged that swept the species to the brink of oblivion across most of the country. The widespread use of a new, highly acclaimed pesticide resulted in precipitous population declines. Birds accumulated DDT in their tissues, usually by eating contaminated fish. A few adult eagles died outright, but DDT's terminal MO caused eggshells to be fatally fragile. They broke before hatching, and with no recruitment the eagle population began to die of old age. In Louisiana only a few survived in the remotest areas of coastal swamps, where in 1960 only four active nests remained. They vanished entirely from the D'Arbonne Swamp, and growing up there as a boy I could only imagine the majestic raptors soaring over the bayou in search of a hapless bass or gizzard shad.

Barely in time, publication of Rachel Carson's landmark book, *Silent Spring,* in 1962 revealed the dangers of DDT and the tide turned, although

it took ten more years for Congress to ban the deadly chemical. In 1973 the Endangered Species Act was enacted establishing the strict protective framework that led to the eagle's recovery. Now more than ten thousand nesting pairs of bald eagles are found throughout the lower forty-eight states with many more in Alaska. In Louisiana, bald eagles are common in the appropriate habitat, and a recent count revealed more than three hundred active nests across the state, a number that would have been unbelievable just a few years ago. This success story has resulted in the bird being removed from the endangered species list, while still protected by other state and federal laws. In the D'Arbonne Swamp they are once again common, especially in winter when the local population is augmented with wintering birds from northern states. In 2003 the first active nest in modern times was found in the forks of an ancient cypress near Choudrant Ditch on the refuge. It is not implausible that the same tree had supported the nests of bald eagles in previous centuries. One chick successfully fledged, and since that time nesting has occurred in the swamp and surrounding area in most years.

It does say something about our country that we don't have to answer the first question in this story. Those citizens realizing the importance of wise conservation of our natural resources prevailed—and because of them our national emblem again soars free above us all. Other similar questions, however, await answers.

On my early morning walk along the bayou recently I was treated with the sight of two bald eagles soaring just overhead before spiraling upward in the brisk air over Horseshoe Bend. The day's freshest light reflected off their snow-white head and tail, a sign that they were mature birds at least five years old. It is hard not to be impressed by their majestic presence, a factor that led to their selection as our national bird. Courageous, fierce, powerful, all of the noble yet anthropomorphic adjectives have been used to describe them. On this same walk I saw other birds. A small flock of green-winged teal, newly migrated from the prairie pothole country, buzzed the tops of the willow oaks. Several swamp sparrows flushed from a patch of high grass on the bayou bank. Small, brown, and nondescript, they quickly dove head-first back into the cover. A pair of diminutive ruby-crowned kinglets, four inches long at best with dull gray plumage, flitted about in a berry-laden deciduous holly. Like the swamp sparrows, the kinglets were probably born in Canadian boreal forests of the far north. Their kind was making this mysterious journey before people first walked along my ancestral bayou.

In terms of value, how do these other species with arguably less charisma compare with the eagles? The question is hypothetical in the moment but not unrealistic in the near future. At one time in recent history bald eagles were by legal definition an endangered species after we nearly exterminated them in the continental United States with DDT. It took a lot of money and clout to bring them back. With bird populations in general plummeting across North America for a number of reasons, funding and the apparent will to address the issues are in a similar, steep decline. Even the Migratory Bird Treaty Act, the century-old foundation of bird protection laws in America, is under attack in a naïve move to enhance corporate profits. For many species, avian biologists are noting the death by a thousand cuts analogy. On our current path, some hapless person with limited fiscal and political resources will soon be forced to make trade-offs and decide how many swamp sparrows it takes to equal one bald eagle. The question could be rephrased as, "Which birds are worthy to exist in the midst of humans?"

Bald eagles were not the only species native to the D'Arbonne Swamp to experience thoughtless and even willful persecution by Euro-American settlers and their descendants. The official minutes of the Union Parish Police Jury for June 7, 1842, noted that bounties of $4 each would be paid for killing wolves and panthers upon certification by two credible witnesses. Within months other records note that a man named William Austin was paid for the scalps of three panthers and another, David Ward, received the bounty for killing a wolf. The bounties were later rescinded, but the widespread campaign to eradicate these predators continued unabated until wolves and cougars (aka panthers) were extirpated in much of their range, including the whole of Louisiana. Today the regional status of both species is complex due to many factors. The red wolf, the historic wolf once found in this area, has been replaced by the more adaptable coyote, the genetics of which reveal a confusing stew of past canid liaisons. Coyotes, such as they are, are common in the D'Arbonne Swamp. Breeding populations of cougars do not exist in Louisiana. On the very rare occasions when their presence can be reliably documented, the occurrence can often be attributed to escaped/ released captive animals or itinerants that have wandered hundreds of miles from their normal home range. Both wolves and cougars have disappeared as functional components of the D'Arbonne Swamp ecosystem, where they once held positions as top predators. We don't know how their demise impacted the swamp. We do know that with their absence the present state is less natural. Unfortunately, even today too many people ask of this situation and similar ones world-wide, "So what?" Aldo Leopold, considered an icon of American conservation, provides an answer, "The last word in ignorance is the man who says of an animal or plant, 'What good is it?' If the land mechanism as a whole is good, then every part is good, whether we understand it or not. If the biota, in the course of eons, has built something we like but do not understand, then who but a fool would discard seemingly useless parts? To keep every cog and wheel is the first precaution of intelligent tinkering."

Before my family moved north to the edge of the D'Arbonne Swamp, we lived for several years in coastal Louisiana near the vast marshlands that were then fairly intact, before the cumulative impacts of the oil and gas industry and busy work of the Army Corps of Engineers coalesced to degrade the most productive expanse of wetlands in the United States. Here as a boy I was first exposed to alligators.

I suppose it could be said that because of an alligator my father almost lost his life when I was nine years old. While inspecting a pipeline from a helicopter in the coastal marshes, he noticed a female alligator near a nest and asked the pilot to swoop in for a closer look. For reasons that were never made clear to me, the helicopter crashed at the nest site. Miraculously, both my father and the pilot survived. My memories of the incident are linked to old Polaroid photographs of the plastic-bubbled whirlybird upside down and mostly submerged in a maidencane marsh.

This event only fueled my budding curiosity of all things associated with the natural world. I am sure my persistent questions led to the wet burlap sack that was dropped at my feet soon after the helicopter accident. The bag croaked. To my delight it contained a yearling alligator, which other than a collie pup for a few months, became my first real pet. Soon afterward, another sack arrived with four brightly banded hatchlings, and a part of my adolescent life became devoted to alligator husbandry for several years. Over time, and in the manner of osmosis, I unwittingly absorbed a good deal of basic biology concerning the reptiles in my tanks. They relished crawfish and dragonflies, but nothing could entice them to eat during winter months. Their senses were such that they alerted to my presence even at a distance. They emitted a pungent musk when riled, and the larger one did not hesitate to attack the small ones given the opportunity. They had strange anatomical features: nictitating membranes and palatal valves. I was only the latest victim of a species that had been beguiling humans for thousands of years.

When my family moved inland from the coast to a hill on the edge of the D'Arbonne Swamp (with pet alligators in tow), I was exposed to a different type of alligator habitat in the form of a bottomland hardwood swamp dissected by a serpentine bayou. Although the habitat appeared suitable for alligators, they had long since disappeared from the immediate area—until, that is, one hot summer day when "Old Grandpap" swam up from the Ouachita River to our swimming hole under the Bayou D'Arbonne Bridge at White's Ferry. We believed the myth that he was at least a hundred years old. He was almost as long as my twelve-foot john boat, and he was a magnificent creature. One of his eyes was milky white and sightless, likely the result of a gunshot. I could approach him on his blind side, paddling quietly to within a few feet, as he floated midstream in deep water. When he detected me, the explosive power of his diving escape was beyond anything I had ever experienced in the animal world. More than a half century later I think that continues to be the case.

Not long afterward, I released my pet alligators in the swamp in Johnson's Brake, Old Grandpap moved on, and so did I. After graduate school on the western edge of alligator range, I began a thirty-year career as a wildlife biologist and manager of national wildlife refuges with the US Fish and Wildlife Service. Soon I was getting paid to work with alligators from time to time. One such early assignment involved capturing alligators in coastal marshes where they were still abundant and relocating them to inland sites where they had been eliminated by overhunting and the sadly common attitude of human intolerance. By coincidence one of the reintroduction areas was the D'Arbonne National Wildlife Refuge, a station that I would return to as manager many years later.

The recovery of alligators, like that of bald eagles, is another of many success stories we owe to the Endangered Species Act. The enigmatic reptile is now common throughout its historical range where good habitat remains. All they needed was protection and a chance to live their lives as their ancestors had been doing for 80 million years. Today, while alligators are present in the D'Arbonne Swamp in low numbers, the population seems stable. Considering the biology of the species and the hydrology of the swamp, I now believe it likely that the D'Arbonne Swamp was never ideal alligator habitat. Lack of abundant food resources and human threats are not an issue. The reason lies in the natural and drastic fluctuations of water levels in this overflow swamp. Alligator nests are subject to "drowning" if the nests are overtopped by flood waters. With extensive flooding of the swamp in most years, successful alligator reproduction can only occur in the infrequent dry years. No amount of well-intentioned wildlife management will alter this situation, nor should it.

There's one small bird in D'Arbonne Swamp that is on the ropes because it is too picky for its own good (i.e., specialized) when it comes to making a living in the midst of contemporary, profit-driven humans. Red-cockaded woodpeckers (RCWs) are small, black-and-white birds once fairly common across the Southeast but rare enough now to be legally protected by the Endangered Species Act. They have evolved to live only within a very specific niche in upland habitats, to wit, stands of pines at least sixty years old (eighty to one hundred is better) with no hardwood overstory and minimal midstory. RCWs nest in holes dug out in large, living pines infected with red heart fungus. The fungus softens the heartwood over many years thus facilitating excavation of the cavities. Walking through ideal RCW habitat, one experiences a stroll in an open forest dominated by large, scattered pines with a lush, herbaceous ground cover. Before Euro-Americans arrived on the scene the necessary "openness" was maintained by fire ignited both by lightning and by Native Americans. Thousands of years of balanced nature (at least in the long term throughout the range of RCWs) crashed head-on into the wallets of consumptive businessmen in the twentieth century, and within a few decades the birds were in trouble. Initially, vigorous fire suppression mopped up straggling colonies by allowing hardwood encroachment into the historic stands. The problem today on the millions of acres owned by industrial interests is that pines are rarely permitted to live thirty years, much less the sixty needed for critical red heart infestation.

Red-cockaded woodpeckers naturally live in isolated clans consisting of one breeding pair and their young from previous years, usually males who help with brood rearing of their younger siblings. The young males stay with the family group waiting to replace their father as the dominant breeding male, while young females disperse in a search for unrelated males as mates.

They use cavities in the old pines as nest sites and secure areas in which to roost at night. Insects are their dietary mainstays, especially beetles and ants gleaned from the trunk and branches of the pines.

Likely never very numerous in the D'Arbonne Swamp, red-cockaded woodpeckers were restricted to the higher elevations that supported loblolly and shortleaf pines. That is not to say that their habitat never floods, as I have caught bluegills beneath the canopy of cavity trees during episodes of unusually high water. Undoubtedly they were once more common when old pines existed. I have heard from local people that when word surfaced of their potential listing as an endangered species, some timber companies instructed their loggers to cut all known cavity trees. In some instances a block of the trunk containing a cavity hole was left standing upright on the stump as acts of defiance—hearsay, but plausible in the realm of endangered species rhetoric.

Today there are three breeding groups on D'Arbonne National Wildlife Refuge, comprising a total of about ten birds going into the breeding season and fourteen after the breeding season. A fourth group near the Bobfield Road vanished in recent years. Approximately six hundred acres of functional red-cockaded woodpecker habitat including cluster sites and foraging areas occur on the refuge. Using prescribed fire, the acreage is burned every three to five years to maintain an herbaceous understory. All other historic RCW habitat around the swamp except one small parcel has been destroyed. Seasonal surveys and banding by refuge biologist Gypsy Hanks reveal that the D'Arbonne birds are hanging on despite being yoked with a grim, long-term prognosis. Two breeding females brought here from Kisatchie National Forest in 2013 to augment the population and provide an infusion of genetic diversity are getting old. (In the past, genetic abnormalities such as crossed bills were noted.) The nearest other RCWs, a single breeding group on Upper Ouachita National Wildlife Refuge, are twelve miles away. Young female woodpeckers from D'Arbonne that leave in search of potential mates likely fly into oblivion.

If there was ever a species of North American bird that lives solely at the pleasure of humans, red-cockaded woodpeckers fit the bill. If ever there was to be a sign of corporate responsibility in an environmental context, it would be voluntary, boardroom recognition that RCWs deserve to live, even thrive, on industrial timberlands within their historic range.

16

Donnie's Gifts—Hurricane Laura—Out of Sight . . .

—Donnie Wainwright came by today, brought a mess of late crowder peas, and told stories. He said that back in the fifties they would catch spoonbill catfish in the D'Arbonne in flag webbing. They would tie them by the tails to green saplings with small cotton rope. At the end of the week when they had enough, they would gather them and sell them whole. He said they were collected at Mangham, where they were stripped of eggs for caviar that went to New York.

He said that his Uncle Rufus once sold three large hickories on what is now Heartwood to three Black men in Monroe who purchased hickories and made them into tool handles.

Donnie said his dad made the coffin for Uncle Forrest and lined it with black crepe paper. He rode with him in the wagon with the coffin to the church.

—Donnie Wainwright came by this evening, brought eggplants, and told stories. He told about the time when my dad lived just down the road with my grandparents. My grandfather Wilburn told dad and Donnie, who were teenagers, to dig all the potatoes in the potato patch one day while he was gone to work. Dad was plowing the potatoes up with the mule when the plow struck and broke a bottle of liquid. They soon discovered buried in the potato hills several bottles of home brew—a type of malt liquor. They drank some and hid the other bottles for later, never mentioning it and never hearing of it from my grandfather. This is first I've heard of my grandfather ever touching alcohol.

He told about a time when he was nine or ten with his older brother Charles when they went robin hunting with a .22 rifle and one box of fifty bullets. Charles let Donnie fire the first two shots—both missed. Charles proceeded to kill forty-eight robins without missing. They cleaned them and made bird pie.

—Donnie came by this evening, brought garden vegetables, and told stories. He talked about Uncle Jimmy Ouchley (Rufus's brother). He said Jimmy was uneducated but very smart in business matters. He made money buying land and selling the timber. He branded the logs and rafted them down the D'Arbonne. He was also very eccentric and later went insane and was institutionalized at Pineville, where he eventually died. He had a large, mean, stud mule that he would ride on his forays. He also had nice walking horses but preferred the mule, which no one else could handle. He drank heavily at times. Uncle Jimmy would ride the mule to West Monroe and come back laden with crock jugs of whiskey and cases of sardines. He also loved to play the "harp" (harmonica) and could be heard coming down the road on his mule before he came in sight, often drunk. He made a wire harness for the harmonica so he could play it hands-free while working in the fields. In later years as he deteriorated he would often blame Rufus for perceived problems on the farm and apparently threatened his life. This feud, his drinking, and a relationship with a school teacher apparently led to his being committed. When Donnie went to visit him after World War II, Jimmy said his downfall was "liquor and that white woman," referring to the teacher. Donnie said he was very smart but also crazy. "He would come and go. He may sell twenty acres for a case of sardines."

—Donnie Wainwright visited today and brought smoked deer sausage that he had just made. He told many stories about watermelon stealing from Uncle Clarence and other neighbors. He told about switching Old Man Alvin Downs's prized seed melon that had been hidden under brush with a small, knotty melon the day before Mr. Downs was to pick his prize and share it with visiting in-laws.

He told of making "tic-tacks" by taking long, thin, pine splinters and sticking them under the clapboard siding on Rufus's house in the dark of night. A two-hundred-foot linen string was tied to the splinter. The boys stood at the other end of the string and rubbed pine resin on it to make a terrific, roaring sound. He said Rufus got after them carrying a coal oil light and his double-barrel shotgun.

—Donnie visited and said my dad joined the Navy toward the end of World War II, lying about his age to get in. After some training and before he was deployed, he was found out and discharged. Dad never spoke of his military service.

He said when he was young they would "thrash" peas and put them in small whiskey barrels for storage. They put Chinaberry stems with leaves and berries on top of them to deter insects. He said this was a remedy of Uncle Jimmy's and it worked.

—Donnie visited and told stories. He said the first modern wagon he saw was bought by Rufus from Reed's in Farmerville. It was a John Deere with solid rubber tires the size of car tires. Rufus was very proud of it and was infuriated when some "unknown" boys took it apart and hoisted the pieces up in a pecan tree as a prank.

Donnie said they grew a strong tobacco that they would cut into plugs and stuff with cane syrup and hard candy to make it more palatable as chewing tobacco.

He said open-range cows would chew up the clothes on the clothesline if you didn't watch them, and as a boy this was his job. (This is the last record I have of Donnie visiting us. He died on April 28, 2014, at the age of 87.)

During a period of four hours beginning at 10:00 a.m. on Thursday, August 27, 2020, the D'Arbonne Swamp changed forever, or if not forever at least for the remaining years of anyone alive today. The change was aeolian in the form of Hurricane Laura. She was obstinate, eschewing the normal shape-shifting impotence that occurs upon landfall, and for the first time in recorded history still maintained a Category 1 status when she passed over and within the D'Arbonne Swamp two hundred miles inland.

Amy and I watched through large plate glass windows in our house on the northeast edge of the bottoms as seventy miles per hour gusts raked the treetops with increasing ferocity—first from the west, then from the east after passage of the hurricane's eye. Surreal showers of leaves fell first like those that turn loose en masse on a blustery autumn day, except that the fall colors were missing. These were still green with chlorophyll. Next to come down were small branches ringed by twig-girdling insects. Then treetops began swinging wildly in oscillations of fifty-foot arcs, and small-arms fire crackled through the canopy as larger limbs began to break. Finally, we heard the abrupt swoosh and subsequent crash of an entire tree falling. All the while, high overhead, it sounded like a dozen 747s were hovering within the gray clouds. I once read that John Muir experienced a similar scene in Yosemite, "every tree was excited, bowing to the roaring storm, waving, swirling, tossing their branches in glorious enthusiasm like worship." Here in D'Arbonne, almost four inches of whip-sawed rain added to the din, but curiously, thunder and lightning were missing. We watched with growing apprehension as our beloved big-leaf magnolia thirty feet from the window swayed seemingly beyond recovery while taunting the wind with up-turned, pale-bottomed leaves like possessed bloomers. Somehow it held tight, and within an hour of the storm's passing we spotted vireos back at work snitching its shiny red seeds as if the event had only been a steamy summer shower. The drama of the hurricane was so mesmerizing that we barely had time to notice the very real dangers. Not one of the old white oaks and black hickories surrounding our house had fallen, instead shedding huge limbs that left us otherwise unscathed.

A quarter mile down the hill in the D'Arbonne Swamp it was a different story. Thousands of trees, mostly the largest and oldest oaks, were thrown to the forest floor. Their tentacled root-balls faced east toward the source of the most powerful winds following the eye of the hurricane. Some were caught in the arms of neighbors, their trunks canted at oblique angles. Many of the larger ones, though, took their leeward comrades to the grave with them like royal retainers at an ancient Egyptian funeral. Their lives had been shared lives. Intertwining roots connected by invisible webs of mycorrhizae dispensed nutrients to the needy and chemical warnings to all when dangers such as attacking insects arose. Scattered among the fallen trees were tall, limbless boles with jagged tops giving the appearance of surviving chimneys in photos of bombed-out cities.

This state of devastation elicits mixed emotions in humans. Some, who view all natural resources in terms of monetary value, see only rotting piles of potential lumber that could have been used to build a new strip mall. They won't be consoled in this case as much of the downed timber is not even fit for salvage because of wind shake, a phenomenon that occurs when trees are subjected to extreme winds, whereby the wood separates internally parallel to the rings. Even if the hardwood market would support salvage operations (which it will not, according to the Louisiana Department of Agriculture and Forestry), most of the trees are useless as lumber. Other people lament the loss of the forest for its intrinsic worth. For those who cherish it as a rich, natural ecosystem, there are reasons to be content, because what appears to be destruction and death is in the slow workings of a swamp actually destruction and life.

Oaks have growth habits that ecologists refer to as "shade intolerant," meaning that young oaks cannot grow in the deep shade of other trees. It is not uncommon to see hundreds of oak seedlings under a parent tree in the forest. Most, however, will never grow taller unless the big tree falls and sunlight reaches the seedlings. This occurs naturally when strong thunderstorms pass over the swamp every few years leaving several blowdowns in their wake. Over time a mosaic of small openings is created across the swamp in which oaks can regenerate for a while until lost to shade once again. It is not an overstatement to say that windstorms are critical to the well-being of the D'Arbonne Swamp. Even though a hurricane such as Laura had not come this way in more than a hundred years, it has surely happened many times in the thousands of years that the floodplain has existed. On each occasion the mega-event causes a reset of ecological succession on a landscape scale as large areas of the forest floor are flooded with sunlight.

So from the swamp's perspective, Hurricane Laura was therapeutic. Young, vigorous seedlings of overcup, water, and, willow oaks were released for rapid growth to become the future forest. Surviving older trees will produce acorns and provide structural diversity in the meantime. And trees were not the only beneficiaries of the storm. The depressions, some

RACCOON (Procyon lotor)

three feet deep, created when the root-balls tilted on edge, serve as critical water reservoirs for many animals during dry periods. Crawfish, frogs, and toads inhabit the potholes and are pursued there by mink and raccoons. The abundant tracks of various other swamp creatures reveal that they often drink from the pools. Violent forces of the hurricane resulted in the creation of countless new tree cavities, a habitat type necessary in the life cycles of many resident birds and mammals. Wood ducks, prothonotary warblers, squirrels, bats, and honeybees are dependent on tree cavities. Even fish, turtles, and other aquatic organisms benefit from a flush of new nutrients and habitat when trees topple into the bayou. Decaying organic material from the fallen trees will eventually fertilize the entire ecosystem from the bottom up. In time, the devastating handiwork of Hurricane Laura on the D'Arbonne Swamp will be lost in another mature forest patiently awaiting the rejuvenating changes of the next big storm.

There is obviously some truth in the old adage "out of sight, out of mind." Humans are a visual species with large areas of our brain dedicated to processing visual stimuli. Most of our knowledge concerning our surroundings is acquired through our eyes. We tend to deem matters that can't be clearly seen as low priority, and for a great many people, if a concern can't be observed directly and unambiguously, it apparently does not exist in their mind. Herein lies a problem as it relates to addressing some of our most serious environmental issues, because they first must be acknowledged.

Plenty of "out of sight" examples are out there. They range in magnitude from the loss of biodiversity associated with industrial pine plantations on millions of acres in rural parishes to the fact that we can't see the invisible, atmospheric carbon dioxide that is causing global climate change. Visually scanning the sky today doesn't reveal rising CO_2 levels caused by our burning of fossil fuels for energy or the fact that the last time CO_2 levels were this high was more than 3 million years ago. We can't see the fish in the oceans to know that due to overfishing, nearly 90 percent of global fish stocks are either fully fished or overfished. Similarly, we can't see birds that are no longer here, this in light of exhaustive research that says there are almost 3 billion fewer birds in North America than a half century ago; more than one in four have disappeared. This particular example makes me wonder how many people could go through a week without seeing a single bird and not notice that something is wrong. And if the COVID virus was as large as English peas, public acceptance of its dangers would be more widespread.

So who or what does see and recognize these issues? Science does—that ongoing, systematic gathering of knowledge concerning the natural world using experiments and observation (though not necessarily visual observation). Robust science can see through the biased cataracts of personal opinions to provide clarity and suggest solutions. That's worth keeping in mind.

17

Swamp Color—Sound and Noise—My Swamp Women

Being aware, being mindful with conscious effort, always proactively sensing one's environs with the antennae available to us, is a prerequisite in order to "see" the natural world. Color is but one characteristic of a swamp that is often underappreciated. Through a windshield, the swamp is brownish-green or greenish-brown depending on the season—all the more reasons to hurry on down the highway and ignore threats to or destruction of this blasé landscape. But for those who look with intent, the truth lies in a natural history of colors.

Abraham Gottlob Werner, a German geologist, was in 1814 the first to compile a book of color charts with examples of each from the natural environment. His *Werner's Nomenclature of Colours* was an important reference for many nineteenth-century scientists attempting to describe the components of nature. No less than Charles Darwin used the book to describe colors in nature on his round-the-world voyage on the *HMS Beagle.* Werner noted 110 varieties of ten basic colors: white, gray, black, blue, purple, green, yellow, orange, red, and brown. He listed a plant, animal, and mineral example for most of the 110 color varieties. In an attempt to mimic Werner's work in a much-abbreviated manner, I offer "A Natural History of Colors in the D'Arbonne Swamp" by selecting only one shade in each of his ten basic colors and using his description with my swamp example.

- "Snow White, is the characteristic colour of the whites; it is the purest white colour; being free of all intermixture, it resembles new-fallen snow." Swamp example: Plumage of great egrets (*Ardea alba*) in angel flight formation at dawn.

- "Greenish Grey, is ash grey mixed with a little emerald green, a small portion of black, and a little lemon yellow." Swamp example: Ribbons of Spanish moss (*Tillandsia usneoides*) teased by summer breezes in the boughs of an ancient cypress.
- "Bluish Black, is velvet black, mixed with a little blue and blackish grey." Swamp example: Flock of common grackles (*Quiscalus quiscula*) splash-bathing on a sunlit sandbar.
- "Ultramarine Blue, is a mixture of equal parts of Berlin and azure blue." Swamp example: Back feathers of a blue jay (*Cyanocitta cristata*) pinching half-ripe willow oak acorns.
- "Campanula Purple, is ultramarine blue and carmine red, about equal parts of each." Swamp example: the pearlescent nacre of the interior surface of bleufer mussel (*Potamilus purpuratus*) shells in Bayou D'Arbonne.
- "Sisken Green, is emerald green mixed with much lemon yellow, and a little yellowish white." Swamp example: the fluttering wings of a male luna moth (*Actias luna*) above the swamp as he seeks wafting pheromones of a mate.
- "Lemon Yellow . . . the colour of ripe lemons; it is found to be a mixture of gamboge yellow and a little ash grey." Swamp example: the fallen star of an autumn sweetgum leaf (*Liquidambar styraciflua*) abandoned by chlorophyll.
- "Orpiment Orange, the characteristic colour, is about equal parts of gamboge yellow and arterial blood red." Swamp example: Cinnabar mushrooms (*Cantharellus cinnabarinus*) shouting out from the leaf litter.
- "Scarlet Red, is arterial blood red, with a little gamboge yellow." Swamp example: the very ripest of mayhaws (*Crataegus opaca*) floating in spring backwaters.
- "Umber Brown, is chestnut brown, with a little blackish brown." Swamp example: fur on the head of an otter (*Lutra canadensis*) appearing suddenly beside my kayak in an oxbow slough.

I have no doubt there are shades of colors in the D'Arbonne Swamp beyond my comprehension in spite of purposeful efforts to seek them out like golden morels. It may simply be a genetic function of time on the landscape. The writer Earl Shorris revealed that "there are nine different words in Maya for the color blue . . . but just three Spanish translations, leaving six butterflies that can be seen only by the Maya." It may be that astute native peoples in the four hundred generations before Europeans arrived here in this swamp saw colors and thus reality beyond those in the palettes of Werner or Georgia O'Keeffe or me.

It is quiet here now on the edge of this swamp, quieter than it has been in many years. Perhaps the level of background noise approaches that when my father was a boy here eighty years ago. I live in the woods off of a rural parish road and almost two miles from a major highway. Even so, a steady barrage of traffic sounds, mainly from log trucks on the highway, typically filters through the trees to persist as an annoying backdrop. It is quiet now because the swamp is behaving as a swamp should behave and has flooded the parish road. Likewise, the flowing backwaters have eroded the foundation of a bridge on the highway, forcing its closure too and the rerouting of noisy traffic. The present lack of man-made noise is beyond just noticeable; it's striking. Visitors from town pick up on it right away. For some, it seems unsettling. Birdsong is louder with fresh clarity. Windsong animates treetops with sounds beyond those expected of the botanical.

In my dad's childhood, traffic noise was an anomaly as vehicles on the sandy road were objects of curiosity that demanded inspection. Other loud, unnatural noises were seasonal and agrarian, such as the wheezing pulmonary din of the small, steam-powered cotton gin that baled the community's sweat and dreams. Across the road from my house a grown-up field sits atop a Pleistocene terrace that was inhabited by people eight hundred years before my great-grandfather cleared the site and planted cotton there. The acoustic environment of humans in this culture we have labeled Coles Creek is easy to imagine but difficult to experience in today's world—the absence of all sound other than natural noises. Even now in the relative quiet of my environment, I can hear a distant lawnmower at times or the muffled roar of an overhead jet. In the history of our species, unnatural mechanical noises are new phenomena. Research indicates they may not be in our best interest from physical and psychological perspectives.

As I am now beginning my eighth decade of exposure to aural salvos, I don't hear very well anymore, the result of too many youthful hours in close contact with heavy machinery and gunfire. In a noisy restaurant I am functionally deaf. I have accepted this sensory loss as it pertains to these situations. What I lament is the fact that never again will I hear the high-pitched, staccato trill of pine warblers on a spring morning. There is balm though in contemplating that the Coles Creek people may have died of old age with perfect hearing.

I have primal feelings regarding the women in my direct lineage with connections to the D'Arbonne Swamp. I'm convinced they have had a greater influence on my sensitivity to the allure of this geographic region than my kinsmen with whom they procreated. Their stories, often buried in the unglamorous files of domesticity, are harder to retrieve. Barbara Ann Jones wed the first-known Ouchley in my family. Dallas Ouchley was a short-lived Civil War veteran twelve years older than her when they married sometime after the conflict. At seventeen years of age she bore my great-grandfather Rufus. Land records indicate they lived on the west side of the D'Arbonne Swamp near the present community of Point. Rufus grew up to marry Lula Susannah Hinton in the autumn of 1893. Around the turn of the century they pulled up stakes and moved to the east side of the swamp, where Rufus and his brother bought 360 acres near the confluence of Rocky Branch and Bayou D'Arbonne. Here Lula had her hands full raising nine children on a hardscrabble farm that proved to be not nearly as fertile as she was. Her fourth child, my grandfather Wilburn, married Theda Armstrong a few months after the backwaters from the devastating "Flood of '27" had receded from the swamp on the edge of the family farm. Their first child was my father. He eventually brought my mother, a south Mississippi girl, to a new house on the south end of the swamp, where she raised a brood while he continued to chase the work of a pipeliner. And in due course my wife, Amy, although not blood kin like these women, has had similar sway on my life. She left her childhood home on the banks of another bayou to merge our lives at a new homestead on Rufus's original lands. North—South—East—West, the lives of Ouchley women surround the swamp.

I know my great-great-grandmother Barbara Ann only through a chair that once belonged to her and was passed along to me. She is said to have brought the chair when she came to Union Parish from the Atchafalaya Swamp or south Mississippi. No one is sure which. The chair is laden with hints and mysteries of lives past. Just a bit larger than a child's chair now, it was originally a rocking chair but was converted to a simple ladder-back when the rockers wore out. The most intriguing parts are the front stretchers. These rungs have been worn to nearly half their original diameter by propped feet, and likely by the same person because most wear is on the same part of the same stretcher—a person who favored his or her left foot. Knowing how hard it was to survive on a small farm in the red clay hills I suspect the mark to be an artifact of worry. However, Barbara Ann was known to revel in the music of her small, round accordion. I would prefer to think she rocked the rockers off her chair and then wore the rung through while marking time to a Cajun reel. She outlived Dallas and a second husband to die in 1925 at the age of seventy-seven.

A cousin remembers Great-Grandmother Lula as fair in complexion with bright blue eyes. A late-in-life photo of her depicts a stern woman, stout in girth, gray hair pulled back and slicked down. Lord knows she had reason to look stern; she was on intimate terms with hard labor. It showed in her large, gnarled hands and forearms, in eyes that plead for the well-being of nine children when the breath of life was more tenuous. At some point when most of her family had grown up and left, when she and Rufus no longer had child labor available to help work the farm and keep up the household, they moved to town and opened a two-story boarding house. Already during these times her lungs were simmering with tuberculosis. She spent a period in the G. B. Cooley TB Sanitarium located near White's Ferry on the highest bluff above Bayou D'Arbonne. Finally, Rufus took her back to Rocky Branch on the edge of the swamp to die. The old dogtrot house on the homestead was in ruins, so her sons built them a small, two-room dwelling nearby. Just out the back door an old tenant shack was patched up for the Black woman Beulah, whom Rufus hired to tend Lula. Both of the dwellings were in the shade of gangly, sweet pecans planted a half-century earlier when Lula's dreams were yet to ripen. She died in 1947 at the age of seventy-three.

Grandmother Theda was an Armstrong from that clan with roots in the Scottish Borders. I called her Mamaw Ouchley and knew her as someone who wore an apron as an integral part of her wardrobe, forever marking her as the caregiver that she was. She tended her kitchen with the same fervor and finesse with which she nursed my asthmatic grandfather, whom she had married at sixteen on a blustery Christmas Eve. She hated snakes and loved to fish. I have a boyhood memory of fishing with her in Bayou de l'Outre with a cane pole so long that I could barely manage it. Her constant warning to watch out for "moccasins" around the cypress knees didn't dampen my enthusiasm to catch the glistening pumpkinseed and goggle-eye bream. When a mud turtle swallowed my worm and hook, she drew a paring knife from an apron pocket and promptly sliced off its head as though it was just another carrot to process. The aluminum roasting pan that she occasionally used to cook a raccoon is now in Amy's kitchen. To my knowledge she is the first Ouchley woman in my lineage to earn a salary. After my grandfather died, she cooked in a college cafeteria and worked as a nurse's aide for years, still giving of herself. She was born in Colsons, the forerunner of Rocky Branch, in 1911 and died in a dreary nursing home in south Monroe in 1993.

The numinous Isle of Skye was likely the territory of my mother's paternal ancestors. She was christened Mae Merlyn McDonald in a south Mississippi Methodist church during the Great Depression and grew up in the Mayberry town of Foxworth, until my father passed through, sweeping her out the front door of the café where she was a waitress and into married life. Chasing work, they moved more than twenty times (in the first grade alone, I attended five different schools from Moose Lake, Minnesota, to New Orleans) before settling in a new house near White's Ferry on the south edge of the D'Arbonne Swamp. There, mother was tasked with raising the four kids as dad kept following the pipeline jobs, returning home during the brief winter off-season. I am the oldest of the siblings and, in retrospect, realize that I contributed disproportionately to her maternal anxieties. One source was the unending flow of wild animals from the swamp that I brought home as "pets." Venomous cottonmouths, untamable raccoons, swamp rabbits with colic, and a great egret in the bathtub that almost speared my eye, were components of a diverse fauna that mother tolerated to some degree. And there were those nights she sat up for me worrying about why I was still in the swamp when the moon had long set and the dogs had come home cowed. She was not, however, always a passive observer of my escapades. As the flood of 1973 lingered into early summer, the submerged vegetation decayed and ripened into a cornucopia for swamp crawfish. It promised to be a banner year for the crustaceans and the many species that consumed them, including us. When Mom volunteered to drag the shallow end of the seine, we launched my aluminum john boat, fired up the 9½-horsepower Evinrude, and motored nine miles up the bayou to the "bean field." Large flocks of egrets and herons were an auspicious sign. Wading into the backwater we towed the twelve-foot net until it became too heavy and we had to maneuver it up on the sloping shore. There were few times in my life that I saw her so excited. The net was laden with hundreds of giant red crawfish writhing one upon the other, threatening us with waving claws. In two hours we filled the boat almost to the gunwales. Mom sat cross-legged on the seat to protect her bare ankles on the slow ride back to the landing. I remember her as worn out and happy in this short interlude from her domestic toil. She was eighty-six when she died in 2018.

Amy, more than any other human, has enriched my life. She and I married at sunrise near a spring-fed creek that is an upper tributary of Bayou D'Arbonne. Our *liebesspiel* had occurred in the swamp as we made excuses to spend the night there while collecting biological specimens for college classes and generally behaved in a manner that could be considered feral if not wild. We are satisfied to have retained those attributes and even to have passed a few on to our offspring. More often than not we still spend our time outdoors working or playing in natural settings. Amy then tends to wear her "short eyes," tuning in to life within reach—emerald mosses, luna moth cocoons, gray tree frogs. I, however, am inclined to "long eyes," searching for a wood duck nest cavity at the top of a cypress or the flag of a doe on a distant ridge. Together in nature we have acted as each other's seeing-eye biologists for five decades.

Edward O. Wilson wrote in his book *Consilience:* "People do not merely select roles suited to their native talents and personalities. They also gravitate to environments that reward their hereditary inclinations." Excepting Amy, I carry the genes of these women in my trillions of living cells. The manner in which some of these genes are expressed is a factor of their environmental exposures. In differing proportions, their lives are now my life. I can see these women today, even the ones who died before I was born, in their lingering daffodils at the abandoned home sites, in the flowing spring where they gathered to launder worn garments in great black wash-pots, in my left-handedness and that of my son and grandson, in the lichens on their tombstones, and in the stories of their swamp connections.

18

*Lord God Bird—Carrying Capacity—Pasaw Island
—Another Hallowed Place*

Lord God! That a crow-sized bird could elicit such an exclamation from people on first contact speaks of a species with ample character, real and imagined. "Lord God Bird" is a moniker for the ivory-billed woodpecker (*Campephilus principalis*), that near-mystical creature and former inhabitant of southern swamps. No other American bird species has roused such passion from amateur birders and professional ornithologists and sparked countless searches for proof of its survival—activities that cost millions of dollars (including land acquisition) for a phantom that no longer exists. Having flown into extinction down the same narrow-gauge railroad tracks that hauled the virgin forests to sawmill dragons, the bird is gone.

The person who was the undisputed authority on ivory-bills, a man who actually cradled one of the last living birds in his hands, describes the largest North American woodpecker in this way: "The plumage of the Ivory-bill is mainly a glossy black with purplish reflections. A white stripe starting on each cheek continues down each side of the neck to the back, where the two stripes curve together to meet in the middle of the back. The outer half of all the secondaries is white, as are the ends of the primaries. . . . The male has a prominent scarlet crest, while the crest of the female is entirely black. The bill of the Ivory-bill is large and ivory-white. The general shape of the bird is long and slender, accentuated by the long and tapering tail." Ivory-bills superficially resembled pileated woodpeckers, a smaller, stockier, and common species that is often the source of fallacious ivory-bill sightings today.

Bottomland hardwood and cypress swamps throughout the Southeast, especially in the Lower Mississippi Valley, once provided habitat for ivory-billed woodpeckers. Their demise was tied to the evolution of specialized food preferences, which included the larvae of certain wood-boring beetles that thrive between the bark and outer wood of dead limbs and trees. Such resources were abundant in virgin forests comprised of many old trees, some of which were always dying naturally. When the virgin forests were logged, the young forests that replaced them were healthy and dead wood was scarce, along with the unique boring beetles that nourished the ivory-bills. Across their historic range, ivory-bills vanished from the cut-over swamps just behind the departing sawyers and axmen.

The last uncontestable occurrence of ivory-bills was in the Tensas Swamp of northeast Louisiana. It is no coincidence that this area was also among the last, large virgin stands of timber in the woodpecker's historic range. Thought to be extinct by some biologists for a number of years, a pair of birds was rediscovered in Florida in 1924, only to be promptly shot by a taxidermist who sold their stuffed skins. Rumors of ivory-bills persisted in Louisiana until 1932 when Mason D. Spencer, a brash attorney and state legislator from Madison Parish, declared in the offices of the Louisiana Wildlife and Fisheries Commission that indeed the birds still existed in the Tensas Swamp just southwest of his home in Tallulah. Unbelieving officials issued him a permit to collect one. In mid-April of that year Spencer shot a male ivory-billed woodpecker on the Singer Tract portion of the Tensas Swamp and hand-delivered the carcass to authorities. Personnel from the Audubon Society quickly confirmed the presence of several ivory-bills in the area, and the news rocked the conservation community. Three years later the first scientific expedition, led by renowned ornithologist Arthur A. Allen II, documented the species with photographs and sound recordings.

The 1935 expedition included a young Cornell University graduate student recruited as a general handyman to help with the labors of working and camping in a remote swamp. In time he became the previously mentioned ivory-bill expert, the person whose image was reflected in the glistening yellow eye of an enigmatic symbol of southern swamps. James T. Tanner returned from the Tensas to Cornell to pursue a doctoral degree with a dissertation focused on the ecology of ivory-billed woodpeckers. Driving a 1931 Model A Ford, he arrived back in Madison Parish in 1937, where he conducted his seminal research off and on for three years. There he captured and banded a young ivory-bill. His work resulted in *The Ivory-Billed Woodpecker,* published by the National Audubon Society in 1942. Sponsors of Tanner's work had an important motive. They hoped to use his findings to justify efforts to save a part of the virgin forest as a sanctuary for the birds and other wildlife in the swamp. It wasn't enough. Even before Tanner left, loggers moved in, felling the giant trees on two fronts. The demand for lumber in World War II accelerated the destruction, and the old-growth forest vanished forever. Tanner's last visit to the relatively intact Tensas Swamp was in December 1941. The last reliable sighting of an ivory-billed woodpecker on the tract by ornithologists occurred on May 9, 1942. James Tanner went on to a long, distinguished career as a professor at the University of Tennessee.

Long after the disappearance of ivory-bills, part of the Tensas swamp was preserved, not so much from logging—a new forest was in the process of regrowing—but from D-8 bulldozers that swept aside the trees, pushing them into torched windrows like funeral pyres so that soybeans could be planted where parula warblers once buzzed. When Tensas River National Wildlife Refuge was created in 1980, I was one of the first managers. Healing the impacts of past commercial logging and restoring the composition and function of a natural forest was a refuge objective. Unfortunately, data on the pre-exploitation era of the forest was scarce and limited to a few published reports. One of the reports was Tanner's work. While poring over his data, I was amazed to discover that he was still alive and in good health. I immediately invited him to visit and share his reflections.

Somewhat reluctantly because of what he might find, Dr. Tanner returned to the swamp for the first time in forty-five years in March 1986. A highlight of my professional career was the four days spent walking with him in the early spring woods pregnant with the swollen buds of cherrybark oaks and sweet pecans while listening to his memories of the forest primeval. At Little Bear Lake he remembered it as ringed with giant cypress trees like "columns of a Greek temple." Only stumps remain. He spoke of two encounters with cougars and a wolf, a "big, glossy black one." At our supper table dining on Amy's venison steaks one night, he admitted that he "was depressed when I saw places where there used to be forests and now are just field. John's Bayou used to be a fine woods." John's Bayou was the location of the last nesting pair of ivory-bills on the Singer tract. Perking up, Dr. Tanner said, "I'm tickled about the refuge, but it is not as big as I'd like." He continued, "These trees do grow fast and

Pileated Woodpecker
(Dryocopus pileatus)

if you come back in forty years, you will be amazed." It will soon be forty years since his final visit.

There is little reason to doubt that ivory-billed woodpeckers once lived in the D'Arbonne Swamp, just fifty miles northwest of Tanner's study area, albeit in smaller numbers because of the size and quality of the habitat. The late George Lowery Jr. one of Louisiana's most esteemed ornithologists, wrote the following passage in a booklet published when he was an undergraduate student: "If the notes of this woodpecker can be taken as a positive distinguishing characteristic, a pair of ivory-billed woodpeckers were heard in the D'Arbonne forest north of Monroe during the late winter and spring of 1931. Several times the shrill, high-pitched whistle, characteristic of the ivory-billed, was heard, but due to the impenetrability of the swamp that seemed to always intervene between the source of the notes and the listener, it was never seen." If the birds were present then, they were on the way out, as intense logging was under way. When James Tanner assessed the forest on May 22, 1939, he described the area as "a small cut-over swamp containing little but saplings where there have been some Ivory-bill rumors, but those I checked up on were based on Pileateds."

The topic of ivory-billed woodpeckers cannot be discussed without mention of the reported "rediscovery" of the species in Arkansas in 2004. Alleged sightings complete with a four-second, grainy video (they are always grainy or out of focus) of a flying bird in the Cache River Swamp set off an unprecedented flurry of activity by university and government researchers to validate the species' existence. More than twenty thousand hours were logged by search teams, but once again the "ghost bird" vanished. Many are convinced that the evidence is sufficient to declare that the ivory-bill sightings are valid. However, doubters among professional ornithologists are common. My opinion was recorded by Michael Steinberg in his book *Stalking the Ghost Bird:* "At our first meeting, Kelby unequivocally said that not only was the ivory-bill extinct but that, in his view, it had not even survived the destruction of Tensas back in the 1940s." Lord God!

"Carrying capacity" is a fundamental term in the science of ecology. It refers to the maximum number of individuals of any type of plant or animal that an area can support in a vigorous, sustainable condition. The availability and quality of food, water, and other habitat parameters determine carrying capacity. It is a concept that is apparently difficult for many people to grasp. Producers of livestock usually get it. They know how many cows the rocky, forty-acre pasture on the hilltop will support in contrast to the fertile, creek-side pasture of the same size. Wildlife management professionals, however, often have a hard sell in convincing their constituents that carrying capacity determines the number of healthy wild animals in an area. For example, deer hunters often want to increase the number of deer on their clubs but fail to understand the limiting factor of carrying capacity. The quality of deer habitat, as expressed in available nutritious foods throughout the year, drives the herd size. Sometimes the carrying capacity nexus is spatially removed. The number of ducks wintering in Louisiana is directly dependent on the amount of breeding habitat available in the prairie pothole region of the upper Midwest and Canada (along with numerous other factors). If a USDA program incentivizes farmers to drain and plant corn in these wetlands, the carrying capacity of waterfowl plummets because the region no longer supports as many breeding ducks—the same ducks that would fly south to the D'Arbonne Swamp in the fall.

Soil fertility often drives the potential carrying capacity of many organisms. Fertile soils grow nutritious vegetation that nourishes other organisms beginning with primary consumers like cottontails and spreading outward through food webs to apex predators such as great horned owls. In a reflection of their watersheds, soils of the D'Arbonne Swamp are relatively infertile compared to the rich delta dirt of the Tensas Swamp to the east. The D'Arbonne soils originate in the surrounding red clay hills while the Tensas deposits are born of rich Mississippi River alluvium. In this comparison, trees and other plants of the Tensas grow faster and larger than those in the D'Arbonne. Their leaves, fruits, and acorns are more nutritious, resulting in a divergence of carrying capacities between the two areas. Thus, a hundred acres in the Tensas Swamp can support half again as many healthy deer as the same tract in the D'Arbonne Swamp, and the trend follows for squirrels, songbirds, and other native animals.

Soil is not the only influencer of carrying capacity. Natural events such as windstorms can set back plant succession, making a closed-canopy forest suddenly amenable to once-scarce swamp sunflowers and yellow-breasted chats. For many ecosystems the most dramatic shifts in carrying capacity are anthropomorphic. Human alteration of habitats, from back yards to vast ecosystems, occurs in many ways. Obviously, converting a bottomland hardwood forest to a soybean field reduces the carrying capacity for black bears, but so does raking leaves in your yard reduce carrying capacity for fireflies (because firefly larvae live and develop in leaf litter). Likewise, the carrying capacity of gray squirrels and wood thrushes plummets when upland hardwoods around the D'Arbonne Swamp are exchanged for industrial pine plantations where selectively bred trees grow in crowded conditions like parlor house pigs. Invasive species alter carrying capacities of native species, usually in downward trajectories, and infrastructure projects like dams, levees, and roads upset that which is natural.

It is a biological certainty that humans are also subject to the principles of carrying capacity. I am mindful of the fact that when the Louisiana Purchase was signed the world population was 1 billion, and when my grandfather was born it was barely 1.5 billion, and that the current population of the planet is 7.7 billion. Already in some areas human carrying capacity for healthy, sustainable living has been exceeded. By 2050 the world's population is expected to reach 9.8 billion. Will we have the amounts of fertile soil, clean water, food, and renewable energy necessary to maintain our present lifestyle? Will our habitats be overcome by our own waste and pollution? Will we become like a mallard hen attempting to nest in a dry cornfield or a lactating doe seeking nutrition in a pine thicket—just hanging on? Some think that technological advances will remedy the issues, but in this realm we don't yet know what we don't know. Dramatic changes are inevitable—all compelled by carrying capacity.

Pasaw Island is out of place, a physiographic anomaly in the heart of the swamp that can push the senses to the edge of comprehension. I came there first with my father in an old bobtailed Jeep stuffed with my three siblings and my mother. My father killed fat fox squirrels with his .22 rifle for a sauce piquante while the rest of us wandered about enjoying the autumn afternoon but unappreciative of our enigmatic surroundings. The place is called Pasaw Island because someone's "Pa" once "saw" a bear there, or so the story goes. A road to the area no longer exists, the swamp having long since repossessed the old logging trail. It is a true island only during back-water floods. At other times it is prominent in its height above an otherwise flat, heavily forested swamp. Rising thirty feet above stands of overcup oak in an area where a two-foot difference in elevation drastically changes hydrology and vegetation, the island is a deviation from the norm. It exists because the bayou that created the swamp by eroding away a Pleistocene terrace missed in its meanderings across the floodplain the parcel of land that we call Pasaw Island. A quarter-mile long and half as wide, it resembles in shape the overturned keel of Noah's ark.

Trees on Pasaw Island are not of the swamp. Loblolly pines, black hickories, black gums, and white oaks govern the overstory. Many are so old as to be senescent and dying slowly as a result. As a boy I would sometimes visit the island by boat to fish when the surrounding backwaters were twenty feet deep. Often the only way I could find it in the ocean of flooded forest was to tie the john boat to a large tree and climb into its highest limbs like a foraging raccoon in hopes of spotting the protruding crowns of the evergreen pines. I had spoken of this place to Amy for years before she got a chance to visit; she was immediately entranced on that first spring morning when we hiked to the crest and were drawn to the ethereal glow of a huge flowering dogwood, as out of place in this remote swamp as a Ferris wheel. For her though, the magic was and continues to be emanating from an ancient grove of tree huckleberries (aka farkleberries). With leathery, lichen-mottled trunks bent over in homage to the elements, and slender, naked limbs straight from a fairy tale forest, they dance on the east slope like a troupe of swamp Kokopellis.

The religion of ancient Celtic peoples included a concept known as "thin places." In simple terms, a "thin place" is a physical place on the landscape where the veil between this world and the next is sheer. It is a place where one easily senses the spiritual existence of Heaven, the signs of its being almost palpable. I am convinced that "thin places" exist today for those who are receptive to the reality of such. It is usually quiet on Pasaw Island, provoking contemplation. The rootings of Johnny-come-lately armadillos reveal evidence of humans contemporary with the Celtic tribes in grog-tempered potsherds. Even at only thirty feet above the swamp, it is light-years closer to Heaven.

There is another hallowed place on the edge of the swamp where I walk in early morning. It slows my pace, wells up in my imagination, and forces me to ponder lives that are impossible to comprehend. Situated on the edge of an ancient terrace, it is skirted by an old channel of Bayou D'Arbonne that has since moved a mile westward. Rufus called the site the Big and Little Indian Camps. With his sons he cleared a few acres of the sandy ground and planted corn and cotton until the fertility played out. Since then the only crops have been a couple of generations of old field pines. It is now known that this remote spot once sustained a vibrant community whose occupants were members of a culture that we have labeled Coles Creek. They lived their mysterious lives here in the D'Arbonne Swamp between 800 and 1,300 years ago. Of their traces, only broken potsherds, mussel shells, fire-cracked rocks, and small, barbed dart points have been found.

When I stand among their ghosts, I try to imagine what in this environment they saw and heard. Certainly it was not the scar of a throbbing pipeline that now bisects the camps. It was not the Japanese climbing fern or the Chinese privet that has followed my invasive ancestors here. However, just down the hill there are large, old-growth trees—water oaks and sweetgums that are dying of old age. The Native Americans would have seen similar trees living out their natural lives. An uncommon plant that I am convinced was here then and that yet remains is yucca. Its rosettes of green daggers are sprinkled over the site. Yucca is often found on similar archaeological sites and is known to have been a source of materials for sandals and baskets. And it is possible, just possible, that a few of the giant, lightning-scarred cypresses in the adjacent brake were young and vigorous when the village was present. The people surely heard the high-pitched, rattling call of the pileated woodpecker as I do most mornings and were familiar with its great ivory-billed cousin that I will never know except in old photographs. When I look up to envision the sky-darkening flocks of passenger pigeons that in their time mysteriously descended from autumn clouds in a roar of wings, I am distracted by the contrails of passenger jets. For a people who considered themselves a part of the landscape, I suspect that the occasional howls of wolves and territorial screams of cougars were more of an aggravation than a source of fear. In that realm I am left with the euphonious music of opportunistic coyotes.

If this is a hallowed place, it once again broaches the matter of spirituality and religion. As mentioned earlier, we have no way of knowing the religion of these Native Americans on the edge of the D'Arbonne Swamp or even if they had one. Based on what we have learned of their descendants after European contact several hundred years later, they likely were intensely religious, with beliefs expressed in some form of animism or sun worship, practices roundly denigrated by prevailing Abrahamic religions. In some parallel universe where the Indian Camp inhabitants could view their home today to consider the damming of the bayou, the loss of passenger pigeons, wolves, and cougars to guns, traps, and poison, the demise of ivory-billed woodpeckers as a result of forest elimination, our definition of paganism would be a hard sell. Perhaps they would respond to that label by pointing to our profane reflections in the bayou.

19

William's Refuge—Trash Fish—D'Arbonne Topogeny
—Magic at The Wreck

Most people who visit the D'Arbonne Swamp are consumptive users of the area's natural resources. On just that part within the national wildlife refuge, officials estimate 4,000+ annual visits by hunters and 20,000+ trips by fishermen. These uses far surpass other activities that are considered "nonconsumptive" in government bean-counting reports. In this category birdwatching, photography, environmental education, and interpretation are legitimate pursuits with their own dedicated columns in the administrative ledgers. For those of us with federal law enforcement obligations, the tidy classification of some visits is broadened. There are illicit drug activities and other crimes, a function of the perceived remoteness of the region. As recorded in my field diary of October 22, 2007, they run the gamut: "[I] chewed out a pair of butt-naked, fornicating litterers at Holland's Bluff." People also visit wildlands for other reasons as Thoreau noted, "There are moments when all anxiety and stated toil are becalmed in the infinite leisure and repose of nature."

William came up out of the D'Arbonne Swamp on Halloween day and badly frightened the secretaries at our isolated headquarters. I received their distress call saying a man was at the office causing a disturbance. When I arrived I found William—medium height, stocky and scruffy, about my age. He had a peculiar stare; his pupils were tiny dots, and he smelled of alcohol. He did not talk much at first but handed me his car keys, driver's license, and a newspaper clipping. The clipping was a month-old obituary notice. William said it was about his favorite brother. William was reluctantly cooperative when I moved him outside and searched him for weapons. Over the next hour, a drama played out that seemed at the time surreal. As I tried to tease out the circumstances leading up to William's unsettling visit, he was lucid one moment and babbling incoherently the next. I learned that we had attended the same high school, and we talked of teachers that we remembered. Occasionally, he would double over in apparent pain and clutch his shoulder. He said a boating accident caused the injury, which he could not afford to have treated. William said he didn't want to be alone now and that no one cared about him. His behavior became more erratic. At one point he asked to retrieve medication from a lunch box in his car. I should have known better. I did know better. Standing at my side he reached through the open window and turned suddenly to confront me with a rusty, eight-inch-long hunting knife—and presented it to me as a gift because I had said I cared about him—this after declaring that he had no weapons of any sort in the car. He rambled about, and I had a hard time containing him. I almost arrested and handcuffed him on a couple of occasions and had just cause to do so. Finally, I had two chairs brought outside and an ambulance and parish deputies summoned. William and I sat in the office chairs on the sidewalk facing each other and held hands as members of the public walked around us going in and out of the government office. There were a lot of sideways glances. William smoked and described the mechanical intricacies of Sig, Glock, and Browning pistols. He said his family had been trying to have him committed to a mental institution—"nut house" he called it. Before the ambulance came and carried him away, William said that he had been living in the forest for several days. He professed his love for the swamp, its solitude, unknowable mysteries, and therapeutic values not unlike Hermann Hesse, who asserted, "Trees are sanctuaries. Whoever knows how to speak to them, whoever knows how to listen to them, can learn the truth. . . . They do not preach learning and precepts, they preach, undeterred by particulars, the ancient law of life." On past occasions, Nature's healing virtues had helped William through the valleys. This time the cure was elusive, the shadows too long.

Humans habitually appraise and categorize all life forms. I'm not referring to the science of taxonomy (the study of classification of organisms based on their similarities and differences) but rather the evaluation of whether a species is worthy to exist in our midst or not. Those that are considered beneficial, that is, those that can be used to enhance our material or aesthetic prosperity, fall into a desirable group. Benign organisms get a pass if convenient. Those that compete with humans or present a physical danger, real or imagined, are usually the targets of willful persecution. We know them by their labels: "weeds," "invasive species," "killer whales," "murder hornets," "trash fish." Of those burdened with the "trash fish" tag in the depths of Bayou D'Arbonne, gar more than any others have been sentenced by unwarranted judgment.

The ancestors of gar originated in the Late Jurassic period more than 150 million years ago. They inhabited North American swamps, along with brontosaurs and plesiosaurs of dinosaur fame, eons before anything resembling an upright primate entered the arena, and they exist today in the bayou just down the hill from my house. Yet we say they are "primitive" because of their elongated bodies covered in armor-like, ganoid scales and long, tooth-studded jaws. With a highly vascularized swim bladder as a supplementary lung, gar can breach and breathe by swallowing air, important on hot summer days when oxygen levels are low. As a result, they are able to live in harsh conditions that many other fish can't tolerate. Gar are survivors.

The cultural significance of gar flows back thousands of years as their remains often surface at Amerindian archaeological sites. The ganoid scales, almost as hard as flint, were used as arrowheads. Early French explorers called gar *poisson d'armée* (armored fish), and farming pioneers used the tough scales to veneer wooden ploughs. One can reasonably assume that gar have been used as food since human contact with the species. Although many people today scowl at the thought of eating gar, their opinions are likely based on the fish's appearance and rumors only. I can attest that cornmeal-battered gar fried and served hot on the bank of Bayou D'Arbonne, while not in the same league as catfish or bluegill filets, are nonetheless quite tasty. "Gar balls" is another popular recipe along bayous farther south. The meat is deboned and ground in a food processor, mixed with bread crumbs, lots of chopped onions, and spices to taste. Shaped into balls, the concoction is then deep-fried in hot grease until golden brown. It is important, however, to never consume the bright red eggs of gar. They are highly toxic and were at one time hung in barns as rat poison.

Four species of gar are found throughout Louisiana. All have long, cylindrical bodies and prominent jaws filled with needle-like teeth that support their predaceous feeding habits. Dark spots cover the body, head, and fins of the spotted gar (*Lepisosteus oculatus*). Weighing up to eight pounds and growing to three feet in length, spotted gar prefer clear, slow-moving waters of lakes, rivers, and creeks. Shortnose gar (*Lepisosteus platostomus*) grow slightly larger than spotted gar, have a shorter snout, and lack their spots. They inhabit large rivers, oxbow lakes, and overflow backwaters. Longnose gar (*Lepisosteus osseus*) have long, bill-like snouts nearly three times the length of their head and can exceed six feet in length and weigh more than eighty pounds. Their habitat is similar to that of shortnose gar but often includes brackish water of coastal marshes. Because of its potential size, the alligator gar (*Atractosteus spatula*) is the most infamous of the group. Individuals exceeding nine feet and weighing more than three hundred pounds have been documented. Alligator gar tend to prefer large rivers, lakes, and backwater areas where spawning occurs. They, like all gar species, spawn in the spring in large aggregations when the water warms. I have found them roiling in the flood waters of the Ouachita River as early as March 15. Several males will surround a gravid female, prodding and rubbing against her to trigger the release of her eggs. Males will then release clouds of milt (fish semen) into the water column that fertilize the sticky eggs, which settle onto submerged vegetation. The eggs and larval fish receive no parental care. Slow to mature, alligator gar don't usually spawn until they are about ten years old.

Alligator gar are by far the largest freshwater fish in Louisiana waters, and adults have a double row of large teeth in the upper jaw. Formidable in appearance, the species has an unjustified reputation as dangerous to humans. The truth is that gar-related injuries are rare and none can be attributed to actual attacks. As a boy I was proud of a four-inch scar on my left calf caused by the incidental swipe of a longnose gar's snout as he flopped around in the bottom of my john boat. The only serious injury that I have been able to unearth was a case of mistaken identity on the fish's part and was recorded in a Union soldier's diary while he was stationed near New Orleans during the Civil War.

There was quite an accident happened to one of Co. F today. He was down to the river washing his shirt. He was standing at the water's edge washing, when a 'Gar' came up and caught hold of his hand. It nearly cut three of his fingers off. It nearly jerked his arm off, he said. The Alligator Gars are a savage looking fish. They have a very large mouth with a long bill running out in front. They look like they could take a man's leg off at one snap.

As is the case with most predators, gar are usually considered nuisances because they compete with humans for other species. For many years fisheries biologists sought ways to exterminate gar that included elaborate shocking devices, traps, and nets. No less than Louisiana's premier conservation periodical once proclaimed, "Economically, the gars are the most important fish in Louisiana today, but in a purely negative way due to their destructiveness" and "the alligator gar is one of our worst enemies of fish life" (*Louisiana Conservationist,* 1951 and 1952). Gar do occasionally eat sport fish, but most studies of their stomach contents reveal that nongame fish such as gizzard shad and invertebrates comprise the bulk of their food. Because of widespread culling, no regulatory protection, and loss of habitat, alligator gar have disappeared from much of their historic range.

Especially when dealing with predators, we are slow to remove old social blinders and look toward the horizon. In many aquatic ecosystems, gar swim at the top of the food chain, a position that often maintains the well-being of those organisms below. Balancing populations naturally is important, more important than eliminating a species, just because it might eat a bass that I might catch one day. And there are connections that we are only beginning to understand. We know that gar eat some invasive species such as Asian carp. Perhaps the most significant role of gar involves their relationship with freshwater mussels. When mussel eggs hatch they develop into free-swimming, parasitic larvae called glochidia. The glochidia attach to the gills of fish, where they obtain nourishment for a period of time until they drop off and grow into adult mussels. Some mussel species only attach to certain kinds of fish. It is important to remember that mussels are the natural filters of our rivers, bayous, and streams. They remove silt and other environmental contaminants, natural and man-made. On Bayou D'Arbonne, the hosts of the yellow sandshell mussel (*Lampsilis teres*) include longnose, shortnose, and spotted gar. Likewise, giant floaters (*Pyganodon grandis*) in the bayou can utilize gar to successfully reproduce. It is not a stretch to claim that a

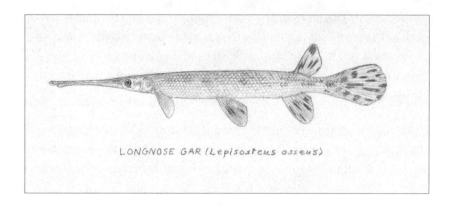

LONGNOSE GAR (Lepisosteus osseus)

healthy gar population can mean healthy mussel beds, which can result in cleaner water for all—a leading role for species labeled trash fish.

On a beautiful summer morning, three friends and I launched two aluminum boats at Joe Bob's Landing downstream of the White's Ferry Bridge. The water level was just above pool stage and cardinal song was in the air. One of my companions was a childhood friend and retired commercial fisherman, who was as familiar with the lower reaches of Bayou D'Arbonne as anyone alive. The other two were avocational historians. Our mission of the day was to put place names on a map of the bayou using our collective knowledge of the area.

Anthropologists have noted that many indigenous cultures developed an ordered procession of place names similar to a succession of ancestral names or genealogy. Each list is termed a topogeny. Oral recitation was a way to maintain and pass along critical information to successive generations. We have no way of knowing what a translated, Native American topogeny along a Louisiana bayou might have sounded like. Surely it would have morphed during the thousands of years of prehistoric occupation. We can, however, create a historic topogeny for Bayou D'Arbonne.

Beginning at the bayou's confluence with the Ouachita River and continuing twenty-seven miles upstream to D'Arbonne Lake dam, we motored against the mild current, stopping often to confer and mark up our chart. The result was a map full of recent history, much of it vulnerable to being lost along with those of us who yet possess the old names. Our ascending topogeny, sinuous as the bayou's channel, included

Mouth of Bayou D'Arbonne > White's Ferry > Dry Slough > Little Brake > Nelson's Slough > wreck of *Rosa B* > Long Reach > Catfish Slough > Gum Cutoff > Cook's Wood Yard > Whiskey Still Slough > Ducote Slough > Cross Bayou > Boggy Bayou > Little Choudrant Bayou > Willow Hole > Big Choudrant Bayou > Steamboat Hole > Holland's Bluff > Big Spring Slough > Long Slough > Eagle Lake > Old Mill > Old D'Arbonne > Lake Drain > Round Brake > Horse- shoe Bend > Jones Brake > The Wreck (of the *Tributary*) > Rocky Branch > Turkey Bluff > Meek's Landing > Francis Creek > Rugg's Bluff > D'Arbonne Lake dam.

Today in a modern world, familiarity of place names on the bayou is inter- esting but not essential. It is handy to convey to a neighbor the location of a good fishing hole or to reflect on the site of a historical event. There is little doubt, though, that indigenous cultures perceived their connectivity to and place on the landscape very differently. The relationship with the geography of their lives was intimate. Such wisdom was often critical for survival. Knowing and labeling the places where mayhaws dropped their fruits in spring backwaters, where the shallow pools of late summer con- centrated fish, where the enemy from the west crossed the bayou on his autumn forays, or the residence of local spirits was crucial. Comparatively, our academic topogeny is one-dimensional.

On another unseasonably cool, late August morning, Amy and I walked to The Wreck, a hike that traversed two ecosystems, and witnessed a bit of magic. From our house on the edge of the Pleistocene terrace where the historical forest was a mix of upland hardwoods and pines, we descended into the bottomland hardwood forest of the Bayou D'Arbonne floodplain. The descent was only thirty feet, but for the biota it was as drastic as three thousand feet on a Colorado mountain. Two months earlier our path in the swamp had been ten feet beneath the natural backwaters of overflow wetlands. There were no signs of the flood today as the forest floor was powder dry; we knew that bluegills and smallmouth buffalo recently spawned where swamp hibiscus now bloomed.

The Wreck is a landmark known to fewer and fewer people as time flows down the serpentine bayou. It is prominent in my family lore. My father told of being taught to swim there by his grandfather before the Great Depression and before cotton sucked the fertility from the marginal soils just up the hill, driving most of his generation away. Tradition holds that when deer finally returned to the swamp after years of persecution, they always crossed the bayou at The Wreck. In February, The Wreck was a favored place to bottom fish for the cold, glistening bass with red eyes. For us it has always been a reference point in the swamp, a location from which to orient one to another spot, a place to begin a story, to reminisce about old times.

The Wreck of course was named after a memorable accident. In 1890 the steamboat *Tributary* sank there after catching fire just upstream at Turkey Bluff. The blazing inferno, fueled by three hundred bales of clay-hill cotton, drifted down a long, straight stretch of the bayou and ran aground in a sharp bend, our turn-around point for the morning hike. Even at the present low-water level, no evidence of the bygone drama is visible now, as shifting sandbars and scouring currents have cleared the stage. In 1953 the boys' Sunday School class at Pleasant Hill Baptist Church organized a scrap metal drive to purchase a water cooler for the church. They borrowed a winch truck and salvaged the last of the iron from the sunken vessel. The bayou on this day was late summer translucent. A white perch fisherman below the bend probed a submerged treetop with a fluorescent jig. Longnose gar breached the surface to gasp the cool air, and an unseen rain crow beckoned an afternoon thunderstorm. The magic of The Wreck, though, defied gravity with wings on this morning. From the exact point of the rising sun more than a hundred wood storks appeared in bleached chevrons of a dozen or more. Escorted by outliers of egrets and herons, and with five-foot wingspans to carry their parcels of myths, the storks, like gangly angels, flap-glided over our heads and over all the stories of The Wreck on their way to tomorrow.

20

Permanence

The matter of permanence surfaced while choosing a tombstone for my father, a task that required unanticipated decisions. Mother and I had decided on a granite stone with a seven-foot base instead of a six-foot one. We liked the natural gray color with rough, scalloped edges. We were prepared with the requisite dates—his date of birth on the hunter's moon, the dog day he died eighty years later, Mom's birthday for the double marker, and their marriage date when "Give 'em Hell Harry" was president. Then came the choices of floral motifs—roses or dogwood flowers. Not having given it any thought beforehand, we naturally gravitated toward the native dogwood that still tries to grow wild around the D'Arbonne Swamp in spite of anthracnose and rampant clear-cutting. This chore, which we had postponed for no good reason on several occasions, began to feel burdensome when we were presented with a choice of backgrounds for the text. Mom chose an open Bible pattern over the scroll style. "Should the names of the children be placed on the back of the granite urn that separates the headpieces?" the salesman asked. "Some do it for genealogy purposes," he continued in a tone that insinuated that we'd be irresponsible should we decide to opt out. After a bit of indecision, we said yes. The gravitas of the matter fell hard with the final option—the "saying." What words should we use to express how we would remember him or how he would want to be remembered? Two pages of single-spaced examples did not help. "It's important because the grave marker is permanent," offered the salesman.

But what, when you come to it, is permanent in the natural world? Permanence, says one authority, is a continuance in the same state or without any change that destroys the essential form or nature. For starters, is even the granite tombstone permanent?

As a rock, granite is indeed tough and durable. Dad's stone originated as a hot, rising mass of magma underneath northern Georgia, just east of General Sherman's infamous trail to the sea 325 million years later. At about nine miles below the surface it came to rest and cooled for a million years. A fusion of three minerals, white feldspar, gray, glassy quartz, and black grains of mica solidified into granite. The monolith continued to rise and erosion wore away the overburden until the deposit was just beneath the earth's surface. Quarrying was then possible.

Using rock drills, explosives, and diamond-tipped saws, a boxcar-size quarry block was hewn from the foundation of the planet. Tons of water cooled, whirling saw blades carved the block into working slabs up to twelve inches thick. Ever-finer grades of emery abrasive smoothed the slab in preparation for polishing with aluminum oxide. More splitting and sawing yielded the final shape of the tombstone. The dogwood flowers and our chosen words were stenciled and sandblasted into the rock. Even though born of fire left over from the creation of the universe, granite according to the craftsmen can also be destroyed by heat.

In a search for the "saying," we considered the permanence of my father's work. I read somewhere that Thomas Edison, pondering his own persistence that yielded eventual success, once remarked, "There is no substitute for hard work." Dad taught this by example. He worked all his life in the oil and gas industry, specifically the construction of pipelines used to transport the nation's energy products. As a teenager soon after World War II, he began as a laborer in the rough and rowdy business and worked his way up to field superintendent. The peak of his career came in the mid-1970s when he supervised the construction of much of the Trans-Alaskan Pipeline, arguably the most environmentally debated project in America's history.

The supply of oil being pumped through Dad's pipeline, though vast, is not permanent. It takes a while to make crude oil—about 300 million years is a good average, which is strikingly similar to the age of the Georgia granite. Most oil was produced in the Carboniferous Period when Alaska's North Slope was covered with swamps, and the oceans were rich in algae-like organisms. As the plants died, they settled to the bottom of the swamps and seas, and were covered by sediments over eons. Increasing pressure from the overburden and heat from the inner earth cooked the tree ferns, cycads, and diatoms until they eventually became a gumbo roux of oil and natural gas. The supply of hydrocarbons is finite because the pot is no longer simmering for a lack of ingredients. We Americans are consuming the oil in form of gasoline at a rate of 178 million gallons every day in order to drive our vehicles 2.5 trillion miles per year. Meanwhile, the clueless monument salesman, in a failed attempt at humor, told us about a local service station owner whose epitaph read, "Ran Out of Gas." Well, true enough. The Alaska pipeline, itself subject to the impermanence of corrosion, may outlast its reason to be.

We buried Dad a mile from the D'Arbonne Swamp in Eocene soil 250 million years younger than Alaskan oil and Georgia granite. The sandy-clay sediments settled out of a vast, shallow sea once covering north Louisiana. Eventual uplifting caused the sea to retreat, and as a boy Dad worked the dirt, tending cotton in a small hill-country field that was grubbed from a magnificent forest dominated by upland hardwoods and shortleaf pines.

The historical upland forests of this region struggled with permanence. Impacts of pre-chainsaw felling had only minor impacts on the rich biodiversity. Small fields were cleared, no larger than could be worked by a pioneer family. Tree species were selected for utilitarian values—hickory for tool handles, red oak for firewood, and black gum for beehives. Twentieth-century demands for building products spawned new technology and a commercial market for certain forest products. Virgin yellow pines, mostly shortleaf pine in this area, were cut and hauled away on pervasive tendrils of newly sprouted, narrow-gauge railroad lines. For two generations the forests survived the whims of the markets with biodiversity mostly intact (excepting, of course, large predators, which are always the first to go). Even when corporations bought most of the land and began clear-cutting operations, the scale of the forests and the resiliency of nature buffered the impacts. Wildlife survived in uncut tracts, and hardwood stumps sprouted anew to maintain species richness. The death knell for my boyhood forests began with intensive monoculture of artificially selected loblolly pines. To eliminate natural competition, the practice involved chemically poisoning everything else in the plant kingdom. It was too much. Chinquapins and blue-stars vanished along with wood thrushes and Louisiana milksnakes. No sizable tract of historical forest survived intact. Permanence is not static. Rather, it can encompass the stability of natural instability involving storms, fire, successional progression and setbacks. Opulent biodiversity is a glorious by-product of flux.

People have been thinking about this issue of permanence for a while. The pre-Socratic philosopher Heraclitus said that the only thing permanent is change. "Everything changes and nothing remains still" is Plato's interpretation of Heraclitus. Plato, though, leaned toward Parmenides, who denied the possibility of change and held that all things are permanent. In *The Way of Truth,* Parmenides explained that appearances of change are only illusions and not true reality, much like the Hindu idea of the atman or soul as unchanging even as bodily forms are altered. Along that vein, Aristotle believed that all plants and animals, as well as humans, have an unchanging essence (i.e., soul) in spite of transforming bodies. Some modern religions consider God's omnipresent love as the only thing permanent. Such liberating thoughts are pleasant to contemplate.

Then, in the midst of tending this tombstone business, news of a terrible accident on an oil-drilling rig in the Gulf of Mexico drifted northward with the spring migrating warblers. Forty miles below the boot tip of Louisiana, pressure control systems failed and a blowout occurred on BP's Deepwater Horizon. Eleven people were killed. In addition to the immediate human tragedy, an explosion sheared off the wellhead five thousand feet below the surface and created a wildly gushing oil spill. Estimates of the amount of pressurized oil surging upward through the casing were hotly debated and often revised. Many considered BP's figure of five thousand barrels per day a defensive lowball. Regardless, in terms of magnitude and environmental devastation it soon became evident that the incident might surpass the infamous Exxon Valdez oil spill—oil that had originated on Alaska's North Slope and passed through Dad's pipeline on its way to the tanker dock at Prudhoe Bay.

Within days I found myself called out of retirement and re-employed by the US Fish and Wildlife Service. I was stationed with others for several weeks on Delta National Wildlife Refuge at the end of the road in Venice, Louisiana. At a near-frantic pace our early work consisted of assessing the wildlife resources at risk, coordinating the placement of protective booms, and managing the overwhelming media interests. Forecasts of approaching waves of oil were always in the background.

The following notes are excerpts from my field diary on May 2, 2010:

11:30 AM—I am writing this from the office of Delta NWR. This second-floor room has large windows all around, and I can see the Mississippi River and adjacent waterways filled with commercial boatyards, piers and docks. The weather is harsh, 23 mph sustained winds from the south with gusts to 34. It is pushing northward a menace that has alarmed the world. It is headed this way. A crisis of unknown proportion is imminent.

12:50 PM—Four large helicopters, like giant dragonflies, suddenly appeared and began landing 200 yards north of this building at the Chevron shore base. One is a Blackhawk, two behemoths carry U.S. Marine Corps emblems, and a smaller one is labeled United States of America. We received word that the president of the United States would soon arrive in his motorcade, driving down from New Orleans because the weather did not fall within safety parameters required for him to fly in the helicopters. A Coast Guard cutter cruises slowly below my window.

2:20 PM—The presidential motorcade arrives, twenty-six vehicles strong, with an armored car, ambulance, and three identical, black SUVs with dark-tinted windows. They pass our office and stop at the Coast Guard station for a news conference.

2:40 PM—Another helicopter identical to the smaller one arrives. Redundancy is obvious.

3:30 PM—The motorcade returns and stops at the end of our driveway. President Obama gets out of one of the SUVs and conducts an informal yet orchestrated question and answer session with local commercial fishermen concerned about the permanence of their way of life. He is facing me wearing a dark jacket and blue shirt with an open collar as he gestures to the worried men in white boots.

3:45 PM—Everyone remounts as the motorcade turns around and drives the few hundred yards to the heliport. The most powerful man on the planet boards one of the smaller helicopters.

3:58 PM—In an extraordinary show of might, the helicopters roar to life and fly north with the wind. It strikes me that they are all the color of oil.

On the following afternoon we eased out of the boat slip at the office in a 29-foot catamaran powered by twin 250-horsepower Suzuki outboards. The big (gasoline-consuming) motors had plenty of reserve as we cruised at 30 knots across the river, down another pass, and out into the Gulf of Mexico. In just over an hour we set anchors on the leeward side of North Breton Island and waded ashore. This place knows of the fickleness of permanence in natural systems. The remnant of a much larger island, it once harbored a schoolhouse for the residents before hurricanes reduced it to forty acres of scrubby mangrove and sand spits. Later in 1904, Teddy Roosevelt in an executive order declared it the second national wildlife refuge in America.

On this day the place was spectacular. Thousands of shorebirds, gulls, and terns whirled and swirled in clouds of wings, some in rigid formation, others beating across the grain intent on life's chore of the moment. Two peregrine falcons slashed through the flocks causing a brief panic. This vibrant pulsing of activity mesmerized us for a while, making it difficult to remain on-task. Our mission involved another species, one that was once extirpated in Louisiana even though it is the official state bird. Thirteen hundred pairs of brown pelicans, not long removed from the endangered species list, were nesting in the island's mangroves. We had come to assess the condition of the nests and the colony in general. Our findings would be considered excellent in a normal year. Most nests had a full clutch of three eggs that would begin hatching in a few days. In short, the colony was thriving. But disaster loomed. At least 200,000 gallons of oil continued to pour into the sea every day. Uncontrollably. On the horizon a sheen of toxic oil rode the crests of waves driven by a relentless south wind, and like industrial pine monoculture in southern forests, threatened even the permanence of natural instability. It was hard not to think that immorality was the cause of it all.

I dreamed of Dad two months after he died. In the dream I was on top of an open shed working on the metal roof. A large post oak grew at one corner of the shed. I heard someone imitating the call of a barred owl and turned to see Dad standing by the tree wearing his old, worn work clothes. He said something like, "It's me. I'm OK."

After the dream, I felt sure that something permanent does indeed exist in the universe. When I think about environmental permanence, it eases the abrasive clamor in today's world to think of geologic time. Still, I have to accept that forthcoming eons will not encompass the lives of my grandson and his future children. At my age it's difficult to contemplate farther. Years from now, Dad's monument will still be around to inspire my grandchildren's reflections of family roots. The wetlands decimated by the oil spill will certainly recover to some degree (although perhaps not completely in my descendants' lives). Outside the boundaries of D'Arbonne National Wildlife Refuge and similar protected areas, forests in this region with historical attributes are likely gone for good. For them the verse that we chose for Dad's grave marker will be relevant as well: "In Loving Memory."

21

Herps—An Old Turtle—Snake Myths—"If You Build It . . ."

Biologists often just call them herps, shorthand for herpetofauna, the reptiles and amphibians of a specific region. The herpetofauna of Louisiana is diverse, a result of our mild climate—one that is ideal for cold-blooded animals—and also because of our great variety of habitat types, from upland forests to brackish marshes.

Reptiles include turtles, snakes, lizards, and the alligator. Amphibians comprise frogs, toads, and salamanders. The two groups differ in significant ways. The skin of reptiles is covered in scales, and if they have feet they are tipped with claws. All Louisiana reptiles lay eggs with shells or give live birth on land. Amphibians don't have scales or claws. Their skin is porous for breathing, and they need to be constantly moist. Except for woodland salamanders, all amphibians deposit eggs in water. Some go through metamorphosis like frogs and toads.

Eighty-seven native species of reptiles are found in Louisiana, including 27 kinds of turtles, 47 snakes, 12 lizards, and the American alligator. Native amphibians include 30 frogs and toads, and 23 types of salamanders. Several species not native to the state have become established here. Herps are found throughout Louisiana, but those parishes east of the Mississippi River have the greatest diversity. Thirty-one species found in this region occur nowhere else in the state. Within the groups of herps, diversity is amazing. Turtles vary from the five-inch-long mud turtle to the leatherback sea turtle that weighs more than two thousand pounds. Flat-headed snakes are less than ten inches long, and coachwhips reach eight and a half feet in length. A cricket frog is barely more than an inch long, and a large bullfrog will cover our dinner plate on a Louisiana Saturday night.

Like coal mine canaries, the status of Louisiana herps can reflect the overall health of our ecosystems including our own human welfare. Many species are very susceptible to the menaces of environmental contaminants such as heavy metals and pesticides. Amphibians have moist, porous skin that easily absorbs toxins. Alligators are apex predators at the top of the food web. As such, they are especially at risk to contaminants that accumulate in those organisms below their level in the web. As shown in numerous scientific studies, the health of herps as it pertains to environmental pollution reflects the same of humans. Likewise, diminishing numbers of herps that are adapted to a particular ecosystem, such as upland hardwood/pine forest, often indicate broad landscape alterations. In this example, it could be the widespread conversion of diverse upland forests to pine plantations. Herps are more than interesting ornaments in the catalog of Louisiana fauna.

A poetry slam was going down at the pond on a recent warm winter morning. I heard it when I first stepped out the front door of my house on the edge of the swamp. Since there are plenty of other water bodies nearby including a bayou and rising backwater, this venue seems to have been chosen expressly for the acoustics. Cajun chorus frogs, a dozen, a hundred or maybe a thousand of them had pulled out their combs and were dragging their amphibious thumbs across the teeth. The theme of the performance was obscure. I couldn't define it at first because everyone was reciting at once. Synchronicity was not part of the show and discordance was rampant. A few leopard frogs scattered among the poets chuckled in amusement at the uproar. Although I couldn't actually see the poets in the water grass, it was obvious they were all facing me, all reading from the same script. As the only human in the audience, I began to sense a mocking insistence in the act. Then their argument, originating in the Triassic era 250 million years ago, welled up in perfect harmony. Their message was that the political events in the morning news that caused me anxiety would vanish like tadpole tails long before the lights on this stage would dim.

Along with the chorus and leopard frogs in my pond, biologists have documented nine other species of frogs and two types of toads within or along the edges of D'Arbonne Swamp. All are carnivorous, more specifically insectivorous, and one, the American bullfrog, will eat any moving creature that will fit in its mouth, including ducklings and turtles. In turn, all of the frogs and toads are eaten by a host of swamp denizens such as egrets and herons, owls, fish, raccoons, mink, and otters. Always a middle link in food chains, they are critical components of this and other ecosystems. Five species of salamanders have been noted, likely an undercount because of their secretive habits. Within the swamp, amphibian niches vary from tree canopies in Wolf Brake where bird-voiced tree frogs chirp in chorus to muddy slough bottoms where three-toed amphiumas forage for crawfish.

Today I held an old, time-marred box turtle in my hand. Could it be the same turtle my great-grandfather Rufus once held on the edge of this swamp a hundred years ago? The possibility speaks of mystical connections. Although the coincidence is unlikely, it is possible.

The most common land turtle found throughout Louisiana is the three-toed box turtle, a subspecies of the eastern box turtle, so named because it usually has three toes on each hind foot. Box turtles have a hinged plastron (bottom shell) that can close tightly against the carapace (upper shell) for protection. Their high-domed shells are about five inches long when mature. Males often have a concave plastron, red eyes, and orange markings on the head and front legs. Females have yellow or dark eyes, duller markings, and a flat plastron.

Most breeding and egg-laying occurs in the summer. Females dig a hole and lay three to eight elliptical, thin-shelled eggs that hatch in about three months. Box turtle eggs and hatchlings suffer high mortality rates. It takes five to seven years for the young turtles to become sexually mature. They are omnivorous and eat a variety of plants, insects, and other animals including flowers, roots, berries, mushrooms, earthworms, snails, slugs, beetles, and caterpillars. They survive cold winter temperatures by burrowing into the leaf litter and becoming dormant. Their wintering site is called a hibernaculum.

Although they may be found in a variety of habitats, three-toed box turtles are primarily a woodland species. Adults have a home range of two to five acres and exhibit high site fidelity, meaning that they don't roam very far in their lives. If moved by humans, they try to return home, an act that often results in their deaths on roads. Other threats include loss or fragmentation of habitat due to development, unnatural fire regimes, and collection for the pet trade. Because of their delayed sexual maturity, low reproductive rate, and high mortality in eggs and young turtles, the loss of a very few adults can cause a population to crash in any given area. However, for those that avoid the hazards, natural and otherwise, they have the innate capacity to live more than a century. I like to imagine the old-timer crossing my driveway and nibbling the mayapple fruits of a late spring morning was also the youngster noticed by Rufus on his morning walk to the shallow well to draw a pail of kitchen water a hundred years ago.

About twelve species of turtles have been recorded in the swamp, their diversity ranging from spiny softshells that bask on bayou sandbars to the terrestrial three-toed box turtles. Others include musk turtles, map turtles, sliders, and painted turtles. The "swamp creature" stereotype from this group is bestowed on the alligator snapping turtle (*trois rang* in Cajun French). Large males can weigh more than two hundred pounds and have a carapace up to twenty-six inches long, a massive head, hooked beak, and strong claws. They are formidable predators of the D'Arbonne Swamp.

Of the six species of lizards in and around the swamp, three are types of skinks, including the broadhead skink whose orange-headed males grow to a foot in length and who are often seen prowling about the cavities of large cypress trees. Others include the ubiquitous, color-shifting, green anole, equally at home on the ground or at the top of the tallest oak, and turbo-charged six-lined racerunners that prefer sandy soils of higher ground as speedways to chase down their insect prey.

Myths that embroil snakes are almost as amazing as the irrational fear many people have of these reptiles. In the United States it is likely that more humans injure themselves trying to kill harmless snakes than are harmed by venomous ones. The myths that persist in this region are as foolish as any.

One tenacious fiction involves the legendary hoop snake. Its proponents claim this serpent takes its tail into its mouth, forms a hoop, and either rolls away from danger or attacks unsuspecting people. Documentation of this behavior is anecdotal at best. Then there's the stinging snake, which supposedly has a stinger at the end of its tail for zapping slow humans. Often the stinging snake and the hoop snake are combined into one formidable comic book creature. In truth, the perfectly harmless and hoopless mud snake is the species usually credited with these transgressions. The coachwhip, a large, uncommon snake of the hill parishes, purportedly lashes people to death with its long, whip-like tail. The scales on its tail do remotely resemble the braided leather of a buggy whip, but victims of such flailings are not known.

At least one myth is downright dangerous. Those who believe that cottonmouths cannot bite underwater best not miss a life insurance premium if they decide to test the matter. Another is that coral snakes have to chew to inject their venom. Snakes don't and can't chew. Coral snakes bite and hold on to inject their venom. Also, snakes will readily cross a hemp or horsehair rope in spite of what some folks think. And snakes aren't slimy. Their skin is normally quite dry, and mostly smooth. When cotton was still grown on homesteads around the swamp, and when a snake was killed in the field, it was often turned belly up to ensure frequent showers during the growing season. Failure to perform this superstitious ritual was believed to court drought. The myths have permeated my family lore also as my grandmother relates the story of her brother as a child being bitten by a "highland moccasin," only to survive because an aunt quickly dispatched a black hen with a single rifle shot, cut the chicken open, and inserted the boy's afflicted foot.

A recent study revealed that some fear of snakes might be hard-wired into humans through evolutionary processes that favored mammals who avoided reptiles. So perhaps people do have an excuse for being terrified of creatures 1/150th their mass with pea-size brains—or is this a myth too?

Snakes of the D'Arbonne Swamp number about twenty species with several types of piscivorous (fish-eating) water snakes being the most common. Venomous snakes include the coral snake, copperhead, and cottonmouth. Timber rattlesnakes and pygmy rattlesnakes live in the higher elevations of the swamp's upper watershed. Most people can't distinguish between harmless species and those that are venomous, an inability that leads to the unwarranted persecution of all snakes. None are aggressive toward humans. As a group in nature's proven schemes of complex food webs and checks and balances, they are no less important than any other, and within the boundaries of D'Arbonne National Wildlife Refuge all are protected by federal laws.

As a career wildlife biologist for more than thirty years, I have long been indoctrinated with the mantra that Nature is best served if we "manage" it. Lord knows I have done some "management" in my time. However, as my on-the-ground experience accumulated, I gradually realized that the opposite is true in many situations. Nature often does best if left to its own devices in its own good time. Restoration work in ecosystems dramatically altered by humans and endangered species recovery efforts can be exceptions to this philosophy. While sitting in my front porch rocker recently, I pondered how odonates might fit into this line of thought. It occurred to me then that another exclusion to my tenet might exist in the man-made pond just down the hill and on the edge of the swamp.

"Odonate" is an idiomatic term referring to insects in the taxonomic order Odonata. They are the remarkably diverse dragonflies and damselflies of the world. Locally, we slight them by labeling them all mosquito hawks. They are characterized by two pairs of transparent wings, elongated bodies, and multifaceted eyes. Before getting down to the species level, scientists divide the order into dragonflies and damselflies. When at rest, damselflies tend to hold their wings above the body, whereas dragonflies hold their wings horizontally. As aquatic larvae and adults, they are ferocious predators helping to control insect populations such as mosquitoes, flies, and swarming termites. Females lay eggs in or near water that hatch into nymphs with gills and hooked jaws. Often dragonflies and damselflies spend more of their lives in the aquatic stage than as adults. At some point though, the nymph crawls up onto nearby vegetation, sheds its old skin, pumps up new wings, and flies off to patrol the wetlands with a vengeance.

Entomology (the study of insects) was a subject that I managed to avoid in college. How could any group of animals without backbones be interesting? How wrong I was! After I left the government, fellow Fish and Wildlife Service retiree Berlin Heck shared with me his keen interest in odonates, and, inspired by him, I began my own clumsy attempts to finally learn something about a group of animals without vertebrae. Soon I ran across several other experts in the specialty. They tolerated my elementary inquiries and mentored me to the point that I can now claim moderate competence in the field.

Twenty years ago I dammed a swale on Heartwood to create a small pond (roughly 100' x 75"). When full, it is seven feet deep. The substrate is fine red clay, and there is virtually no emergent vegetation. After I observed the pond for a couple of years, it became obvious that the watershed was too small and the droughts now too frequent to keep the pond filled year-round. It often evaporates to a depth of two feet in the summer and fall. For this reason I decided not to introduce fish to the pond. Still, it does provide good wildlife habitat for a host of species that includes deer, raccoons, squirrels, several aquatic turtles and snakes, and many types of birds. During my odonate tutelage, the Heartwood pond also served as an excellent laboratory to study those insects. I continue to keep a close watch on the area and have photo-documented five species of damselflies and thirty-seven species of dragonflies. I list them here if for no other reason than to display a sample of their fantastic common names.

Damselflies

Lestes australis	Southern Spreadwing
Enallagma doubledayi	Atlantic Bluet
Enallagma aspersum	Azure Bluet
Ischnura posita	Fragile Forktail
Ischnura hastate	Citrine Forktail

Dragonflies

Tachopteryx thoreyi	Gray Petaltail
Nasiaeschna pentacantha	Cyrano Darner
Anax junius	Common Green Darner
Arigomphus lentulus	Stillwater Clubtail
Arigomphus maxwelli	Bayou Clubtail
Gomphus oklahomensis	Oklahoma Clubtail
Gomphurus hybridus	Cocoa Clubtail
Dromogomphus spinosus	Black-shouldered Spinyleg
Cordulegaster oblique	Arrowhead Spiketail
Didymops transversa	Stream Cruiser
Macromia illinoiensis	Swift River Cruiser

Epitheca cynosure	Common Baskettail
Epitheca princeps	Prince Baskettail
Epitheca semiaquea	Mantled Baskettail
Plathemis Lydia	Common Whitetail
Ladona deplanata	Blue Corporal
Libellula auripennis	Golden-winged Skimmer
Libellula cyanea	Spangled Skimmer
Libellula luctuosa	Widow Skimmer
Libellula flavida	Yellow-sided Skimmer
Libellula incesta	Slaty Skimmer
Libellula semifasciata	Painted Skimmer
Libellula vibrans	Great Blue Skimmer
Orthemis ferruginea	Roseate Skimmer
Perithemis tenera	Eastern Amberwing
Celithemis elisa	Calico Pennant
Celithemis fasciata	Banded Pennant
Erythemis simplicicollis	Eastern Pondhawk
Erythrodiplax minuscula	Little Blue Dragonlet
Erythrodiplax umbrata	Band-winged Dragonlet
Pachydiplax longipennis	Blue Dasher
Sympetrum ambiguum	Blue-faced Meadowhawk
Tramea carolina	Carolina Saddlebags
Tramea onusta	Red Saddlebags
Tramea lacerate	Black Saddlebags
Pantala flavescens	Wandering Glider
Pantala hymenaea	Spot-winged Glider

My documentation of the azure bluet is the only record of that species in Louisiana, and the Stillwater clubtail is the first state record (others have been found since). That I've never been able to find some common species on the list such as Oklahoma clubtail and calico pennant away from the small pond in the vastly larger D'Arbonne Swamp speaks to the specialized requirements of certain odonates. Likewise, blue-fronted dancers and blue-tipped dancers are abundant on the bayou's edge several hundred yards from my pond but absent here. I don't know why particular odonates are attracted to the pond. I often see various species patrolling territory, mating, ovipositing (laying eggs), and foraging here. Perhaps the absence of predatory fish is a factor. I suspect the reason is more complex and involves more details than exist in our current state of knowledge.

Before the pond was built it would have been difficult to record a half dozen transient species of odonates on the dry upland site. So does this mean that if you build (i.e., "manage") it, they will come? Perhaps, in some cases with some species. As a general precept though, given the option, it's wiser to protect existing natural areas along with their native flora and fauna, and let Nature carry on, rather than rely on the dangerous premise that we can reconstruct via "management" all those we destroy.

22

A Walk in the Dark—Deer in the Woods—Nocturnal Migration —The Avian Crisis

As a species we have never liked the dark. For several hundred thousand years we have retreated to caves and other shelters, huddled closer to blazing fires, and shouldered a heavier burden of anxiety after sunset. Predators real and imagined lurked in the shadows; denizens of the spirit world had their way after dark. Everyone had stories of bad things that happened when the vital sense of vision was rendered impotent at night.

Nothing much has changed today. In Louisiana where many are familiar with our forests and swamps, the idea of being in their midst at night without an artificial light of some sort is not appealing. Even with the rational knowledge that predators of humans no longer exist here (except those of our own ilk), a survival memory deep within our brain still tugs us back to the campfire.

In the same manner, natural sounds made by nocturnal animals elicit unique feelings in humans. Exposure to the otherworldly cries of mating foxes has caused frissons in many. Haunting calls of great horned owls and the hell-borne screams of barred owls can produce terror in otherwise stoic individuals. All contribute to our wariness of darkness.

As creatures of light, humans are in the minority. Most animals, except birds not including owls, are partially or completely nocturnal. Where we are uneasy, animals find succor in shadows, perhaps sensing that this is the time when we humans in our roles as apex predators are least likely to threaten.

People who lived around the D'Arbonne Swamp were not spared the hardships of the Great Depression. Cousin Lea said the Ouchley family, like many others, had to "root-hog or die" in those times. Gardens, free-ranging livestock, and prayers provided sustenance, and few went hungry even though money was scarce as a tame wildcat. The swamp also made contributions to human larders with fish, bullfrogs, squirrels, ducks, robins, raccoons, 'possums, and mayhaws.

One of my father's boyhood tasks was providing rabbits for the supper table. He hunted them on dark nights when they were most likely to be out and about. In this time before portable batteries, carbide lanterns were required for the hunt. They were finicky contraptions with a lower compartment to contain the calcium carbide and an upper reservoir that was filled with water. When the water dripped onto the calcium carbide through a valve, acetylene gas was produced. Igniting the gas yielded a flame in front of a reflector that projected the light forward. Rabbits were detected by their eyeshine in the dim glow of the light. Boys new to the venture were reminded that because rabbits' eyes are on the side of their head, only one eye could be seen at a time. And if, when walking alone through the swamp at night, a person were to spot two eyes shining, he should be aware that such anatomy is a trait of many predators that can see much better at night than a mere boy.

Upon hearing these stories and in the way of a naïve boy, I yearned for the night when I could try my hand at such adventure. Parental resistance was reluctantly waived when I turned thirteen, and I made plans. Of course, night hunting was illegal, so my idea was to hike down the road toward White's Ferry and slip into the woods on a path that led to Johnson's Brake, a beautiful stand of flooded cypress and water tupelo trees that hugged the foot of the hills above the swamp. I would hunt along the trail between the hills and brake until midnight or until I had all the rabbits I could carry. I chained Sergeant, our German shepherd, to a clothesline pole to keep him from tagging along. The brick-like, six-volt battery that powered my headlamp went into the pocket of my hunting vest. This rig was the successor to carbide lanterns. I carried Dad's old single-shot, 20-gauge shotgun. This was the same gun I killed my first deer with—the one with the broken shell

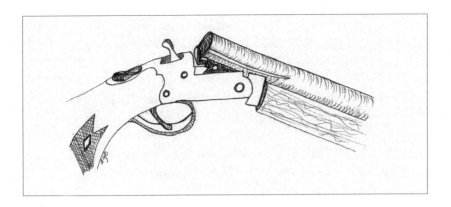

extractor, which required a long, green stick to jam down the barrel to remove the spent shell. A sandwich, a sheath knife to gut my game, and a
box of short brass, paper-hulled shotgun shells (Peters brand) loaded with
number 7½ lead shot completed my trappings.

The autumn evening was cool and starlit. To save on battery power, I
didn't turn on my headlamp until I reached the edge of the brake, when
abruptly I was surrounded by the white, diamond-like glow of eyes in every direction. They were, I cautiously determined, the eyes of spiders also
out for a night's hunt. Continuing on down the path, I walked for an hour
before stopping to eat my sandwich on a fallen log. I had seen a total of one
rabbit, which disappeared before I could align the light beam along my gun
barrel. The reflection from its eye was a soft glow, not at all like those of the
spiders. Still, the forest was beautiful that evening. Water in the brake to the
right of the path was dark and translucent, a result of tannin-laden leaves
that fell from overhanging trees—leaves that were slow to decay on the
anaerobic bottom. A pure stand of cypress and water tupelo trees flaunted
broad, tapering trunks—a characteristic of their species when growing on
sites flooded most of the year. Almost a half century later I would learn that
cavities in these two species in the D'Arbonne Swamp were essential habitat for rare Rafinesque's big-eared bats. To the left of the trail, the hillside
was clothed in a diverse upland forest rife with dozens of species of trees,
shrubs, and vines. My path was an ecotone, a transitional area between two
ecological communities.

Mesmerized by the atmosphere of the forest at night, I lingered until roused by a stirring in the leaves beyond the range of my headlamp. I walked on down the trail, encouraged and thinking the rabbits were perhaps only now beginning to move. They were not. I saw nothing in the next half mile, even though I occasionally heard rustling noises in the darkness. By now my headlamp was beginning to dim, and it dawned on me that the sounds in the shadows were becoming more frequent and were always behind me. At that point I decided to turn around and backtrack to civilization before my light completely failed. Flanked by the brake and hills, I wasn't worried about getting lost without a light, but I was convinced something was following me. The sound of footfall in the dry, autumn leaves would stop when I stopped. Each time I stopped, I quickly spun around with my light—nothing. As my headlamp grew dimmer and dimmer, the forest shadows came closer. My pursuer was closer too and matched my pace step for step as long as I was moving. Youthful imagination is as flammable as broomsedge straw, and by then I could no longer look behind for fear of confronting a pair of glowing predator eyes. I couldn't manage to run either, not that it would have mattered. When I didn't think I could endure another moment, a heavy weight crashed onto my back, huge hairy paws gripped my shoulders, and I fell to the ground with a moan. The creature's wet tongue on the back of my neck finally brought me around. Convinced that he was forgiven for slipping his collar and tracking me in the swamp, Sergeant, my intractable dog, was as eager to make amends as I was to thrash him with my green ramrod stick that had vanished in the commotion.

More than fifty years after the misadventure with Sergeant I walked across the street from my house on the north edge of the D'Arbonne Swamp and killed a deer late one afternoon. The land here is in the process of producing its third forest in historic times. One hundred years ago my great-grandfather tried to feed his large family by growing corn and cotton on the marginal soils. Eventually they pretty much starved out, and it was a toilsome life for those in my grandfather's generation. One thing is certain. Neither of these close relatives could have supplemented their diet with venison backstraps from the property as I did. In their day deer had been eliminated from this area and indeed from much of the eastern United

States. The species that had once played the same vital role for eastern Native American cultures as bison did for those in the West survived only in the most remote and inaccessible regions. Habitat modification and large-scale, unregulated hunting initiated a population plunge that ended only in the early twentieth century.

The onset of scientific wildlife management, including applied research and restrictive harvest regulations, resulted in a dramatic recovery of the species. At an estimated population of 30 million, more white-tailed deer live in North America now than at any time in the past. Last year (2018–19) in Union Parish where I shot the deer, hunters harvested 3,794 deer, or one deer per 126 forested acres. The total harvest for all Louisiana was 120,800. For hunters the resurgence of deer has been a welcome phenomenon.

The news though is not all good these days. Deer populations in many areas of the country are now unnaturally high and unsustainable. Deer predators no longer exist in numbers sufficient to keep herds in balance with habitat. Hunting as a management tool to keep populations in check is declining. Managers are concerned that widespread habitat destruction and die-offs may occur in some regions.

Even in Louisiana there has been a steady downward trend in deer harvested over the last ten years. Areas of concern include declining lactation rates in does, indicating reproductive issues caused by some form of stress (e.g., nutritional, flooding, poor habitat); competition with increasing feral hog populations; loss and degradation of good habitat due to development and such practices as industrial pine tree farming; and the threat of chronic wasting disease. If at some point venison backstraps once again become scarce in the D'Arbonne Swamp, it will likely be because of a different type of habitat destruction than the first time around, and a lack of hunting instead of too much.

Beneath the wings of Cassiopeia they rise in a cloud at dawn from the Arctic tundra of La Perouse Bay to ride the back draft of a cold front racing toward the Gulf of Mexico. Circling for altitude, clusters break away to form chevrons of miracles. Old birds, knowing well the aroma of Lacassine marshes 2,000 miles down the aerial highway, beat the path barking orders to youngsters who gabble excitedly among themselves. On this voyage the secrets of survival are borne on snow-white wings dipped in midnight; remembrances of the past are wrapped in downy breasts. Bearing runes of creation in a genetic code that defies illumination, they fall from the welkin onto our wetlands as handsels from God.

The florid paragraph above describes the autumn migration of snow geese, much of which occurs at night. When I invite friends to go birdwatching along Bayou D'Arbonne in the middle of the night, they immediately suspect shenanigans of the mythical snipe hunt. However, that is not the case as there are opportunities to birdwatch at night in Louisiana. September and October are some of the best times. During this period, fall migration is in full swing, and it is common to see flocks of hawks, vultures, and pelicans riding the afternoon thermals. These birds that soar and glide on fixed wings usually migrate during the day to take advantage of vertical updrafts generated when the sun heats the earth. But birds that employ wing-flapping flight generally migrate at night. Most songbirds, shorebirds, and many waterfowl travel under the cover of darkness.

For years, nocturnal migration was thought to be an adaptation to allow birds to avoid predators or to effectively navigate using the stars. Neither of these theories explains the behavior for all species. Many large birds such as herons, ducks, and geese are rarely at risk from avian predators, and flights of these species on cloudy, starless nights are common. Recent theories suggest that nocturnal migration is based on atmospheric conditions. During the day, the atmosphere is less stable as the sun heats the earth. Airplane passengers frequently experience bumps and jolts due to turbulence. Imagine the effect on a two-ounce songbird. After dark, thermal activity ceases, the air smooths, and small birds can travel more efficiently. Air temperature also affects flight. Flapping wings generate body heat, and birds must be careful not to overheat. Flying at night when the air temperature is cooler is an advantage. Radar studies along the coast convey the scope of nocturnal migration in Louisiana. During peak migration, up to 50,000 songbirds per hour pass through each linear mile scanned by radar.

This phenomenon is best experienced on a bright, moonlit fall night. A half to full moon is best. Focus a pair of high-powered binoculars, or better yet a telescope, on the disc of the moon, and watch for dots that move across the moon's face. Sometimes faint birdcalls can even be heard—messages from avian travelers responding to ancient urges.

An article recently published in the journal *Science* rattled the American conservation community like no other. The paper summed up the results of multifaceted research by the premier avian science groups in the country. It included analyses of years of breeding population data on 529 species of birds, many of which are at home in the D'Arbonne Swamp at some point in their life cycle. Additionally, it considered decades of radar data that track bird migrations. It's the best science that exists, and it declares there are almost 3 billion fewer birds in North America than there were forty-eight years ago; more than one in four have disappeared.

Breaking down the data revealed more surprises. Birds from many different groups are declining in many different habitats, not just forest birds or birds that were scarce to begin with. The list includes wood thrushes, white-crowned sparrows, meadowlarks, and the juncos that once swarmed under our Heartwood feeders. The study also indicates that the trend may be getting worse as there has been a 14 percent decrease in nocturnal spring migrants in just the last ten years. Determining cause of the declines was not within the scope of the study, but researchers point toward evidence in other work that reveals a number of issues: habitat loss on many fronts; climate change; the reality that our world is awash in pesticides that kill insects and plants vital to birds; outdoor cats; collisions with buildings and other structures.

So what can be done? Birding organizations have recommended helpful practices for everyone: avoid pesticides; use native plants in your landscape (instead of sterile, high-maintenance lawns); keep cats indoors; make windows safer for birds; reduce plastic use (and thus the need for oil and gas development in bird-sensitive areas); drink shade-grown coffee (to reduce the need to clear tropical forests for coffee growing). Also at this critical time in our history when we seem to be rushing toward a number of cliffs beyond which the natural world will cease to exist as humans know it, the most effective approach may be political action. When we should be doubling down to start new initiatives to help birds, we have instead seen in recent years assaults from Washington on the Migratory Bird Treaty Act, the Endangered Species Act, and other regulations and policies that have long benefited birds. It is imperative that decision-makers are not science-averse and are capable of understanding that our well-being is inseparably tied to the well-being of the natural world.

It is encouraging that most of the people involved in this study believe the declines can be stopped in most cases and that populations can recover, at least to some extent, if there is a collective will to address the calamity. We have good examples. The continental waterfowl population has increased markedly since 1970, primarily because of proactive, large-scale wetland conservation efforts. Likewise, once imperiled raptors such as bald eagles are thriving since the ban on DDT took place. The measure of the problem now though is more complex, the potential outcome more ominous. It will not be solved unless a majority moves beyond the hand-wringing stage.

23

Tree Chatter—"Holey" Trees—Letter to a Red Oak—
My Bayou Antithesis—Living Purposefully

Adjacent to the swamp and at the top of my long driveway through a patch of diverse forest that is at least 130 years old, there was a peculiar episode of mortality not long ago. The deaths involved three large trees that, up until the time their leaves withered and transpiration failed, appeared healthy. They all died within a two-month period. The victims were within forty feet of each other, and though there were many others nearby, none were affected. Adding to the mystery was the fact that the trees were of three different species—a white oak, a mockernut hickory, and a southern red oak. Other than a couple of recent droughty summers that likely stressed the forest to some degree, common causative signs of tree deaths were absent the scene. Evidence of lightning strikes, injurious insects, diseases, or chemical poisoning was missing. However, recent discoveries involving plants' ability to communicate offer a plausible explanation.

We now know that trees have an intelligence of sorts that includes relationships with others of their own kind and even different species. Intelligence is expressed in their abilities to communicate with soil bacteria and fungi. Tree roots converse with fungi, sending chemical messages through the soil that attract fungi and stimulate them to grow toward the roots. Root and fungus then exchange sugar and minerals for their mutual benefit. In a mature forest a mesh of fungi develops that connects the root tips of adjacent trees like a botanical fiber optic network. Through this system, trees can send nutrients and chemical messages to each other. A tree attacked by insects can communicate this to nearby trees via the root/fungi network, resulting in the neighbors' fortifying their own leaves with insect deterring chemicals. A weak, shade-stunted sapling can obtain nourishment from a parent tree whose higher boughs manufacture an abundance of sugar via photosynthesis.

As for my three trees, they were friends in something more than a metaphorical sense. They grew up together and lived side by side for over a century. They communicated, warned each other of dangers, and helped their cohorts in hard times. I surmise that for some unknown reason, perhaps drought on top of old age, one of the trees died. By then the lives of all three were so intertwined beneath the ground that the other two could not survive the loss and they perished also. It is hard for many people, especially those of us with hard science backgrounds, to think of plants in this manner with abilities and senses so foreign to our views, to accept that in essence plants "talk" among themselves. I suspect that in this field at this time, we don't even know what we don't know.

The title of this short essay could be "Holey Trees." It is not about the spiritual aspects of a forest (i.e., "Holy Trees") but rather the presence or absence of cavity trees in a forest. In the realm of commercial forestry, trees with holes are undesirable. They take up space where more valuable, sound trees can grow. For that reason cavity trees have been all but eliminated on millions of acres. It's that money thing.

But in southern woodlands, trees with cavities once occurred naturally across the landscape. Cavities form when trees are injured or diseased; also, animals, especially woodpeckers, excavate holes in living and dead trees. As vital components of a forest, cavity trees provide nesting, roosting, and denning habitat for many types of wildlife. At least eighty-five species of birds in North America are dependent on cavities. In and around the D'Arbonne Swamp many of our most popular birds nest in cavities, including the eastern bluebird, Carolina wren, Carolina chickadee, tufted titmouse, prothonotary warbler, tree swallow, purple martin, and wood duck. Most owls in the United States nest in cavities. These species are secondary cavity nesters in that they don't excavate their own holes but rather use those made by woodpeckers or other natural causes such as decay. It is ironic that many of these species, whose populations decline when cavity trees are removed, are also insectivorous and play an important role in controlling forest insect pests.

Local mammals are also dependent on tree cavities. Squirrels, opossums, raccoons, skunks, mink, and gray foxes den in tree hollows. Research on area wildlife refuges has revealed Rafinesque's big-eared bats, which also help control harmful insect populations, prefer to roost in hollow water tupelo trees. Large, hollow cypress trees have been identified as important denning and birthing sites for Louisiana black bears.

Even though appropriate man-made nest boxes designed for particular species can be beneficial on a small scale, the obvious answer to this conservation dilemma is to promote and preserve naturally occurring cavity trees. Research indicates two to three such trees per acre can enhance biodiversity and foster healthy forests. Holey trees are not without value.

Dear Red Oak near the Gate,

I'm not going to be so presumptuous as to tell you your business, like how to grow or how not to grow all spraddled out like that. You've been around almost twice as long as I have and obviously know a thing or two about how to get along in this world. Homesteading so close to the road, you've seen a lot. I'm sorry to say that it was likely my great-grandfather Rufus who began contributing to the soil compaction over your roots when he bought the first modern wagon in this area, a John Deere with solid rubber tires. But upland hardwood trees were common around here in those days, and folks needed shade. Then it was my grandfather with his nineteen twenty-something Star automobile with big, brass headlights, the first car on the sandy, one-track road. My dad followed up with post-World War II Fords. Like you, they had to work hard or die on this hill just up from the D'Arbonne Swamp. Unlike you, they moved on to more fertile ground when the cotton played out. I'm a late comer to this picture and only a few years ago acquired a piece of paper that declares you live on my property. Now that is presumptuous considering that I live on your land.

When I moved out here on your property and built a cypress house, I brought a mental sack full of classical Latin names that I had gathered up from universities near and far. Yours is *Quercus falcata,* which means oak tree with leaves that have sickle-shaped lobes. Since we are acquaintances, I prefer to address you with the more familiar term—Southern Red Oak. I walk past you most days on my morning hike and often wonder about your life. What caused the injury that led to the small hollow on your east side? How much metal is hidden beneath your dark furrowed bark in the form of iron nails, rusty barbed wire, and lead bullets? Is the air more polluted now than in your youth? Did Uncle Jimmy ever tie his giant black mule to your low limbs after he had ridden across the swamp from Trenton laden with a case of sardines and an empty whiskey bottle or two as the stories say? How have you managed to dodge lightning bolts all these years? Since we have a lot in common, including 70 percent of our DNA, I suppose the essence of those questions could be asked of me one day.

As a prominent citizen around here, you are well-known to a lot of other life forms in the area. Poison ivy and Virginia creeper vines use you for a trellis. I have seen blue jays and cat squirrels pinching your acorns on occasion. Orchard orioles hang their bag nests high in your boughs. A swamp rabbit seeks shelter in the ground-level cavity at times, and in your forks resurrection fern withers and revives in cyclic worship of the weather. I realize too that everyone is not on the best of terms, as it is obvious that you and an old, recently deceased walnut tree had subsoil run-ins over the rights to scarce nutrients; you apparently won that quarrel. Nonetheless, you are a good example of how to age well, get along with others when you can, stand your ground in spite of adversity, and still flower as senescence approaches. I aspire to that.

For at least forty years I have spent several weeks each year in places where the word "bayou" is unfamiliar to most people. The maps there don't have names like "D'Arbonne," "de L'Outre," or "Teche." There are no such streams with their characteristic side-dressing of cypress trees and Spanish moss for a thousand miles. No alligators or alligator gar; no smothering Louisiana humidity.

It is not as if those distant places lack water. Although scarce when compared to our saturated landscapes, it exists in geologically young channels with tails atop snow-capped mountains and sweeps downward through sagebrush deserts, all the while yielding more elevation in a mile than Bayou D'Arbonne does in its entirety. The watercourses range in size from creeks to rivers. Out west, water moves ceaselessly, second only to the wind. Those stretches without dams and reservoirs host lush riparian oases of cottonwoods and willows along with rich biodiversity that rivals that of a southern swamp. Here are cutthroat trout, sage grouse, trumpeter swans, and moose. Here are the vital nesting and refueling refuges of the very birds that fly up our bayous in the spring and down them each autumn—yellow warblers, blue-winged teal, cedar waxwings, white-crowned sparrows. . . . On dark nights, the raucous insect and frog noise of bayous is absent, but brilliant starscapes unfettered by light pollution reflect in the western streams and are the backdrop for sounds of individual creatures—an adolescent coyote's hungry yelps, a sandhill crane's soft, rattling crow, and the call that stirs emotions like no other—the plaintive howl of lobo with Leopold's fierce green fire still hot in her eyes.

I am now back on the edge of a Louisiana swamp and just up the hill from a bayou where my great-grandfather taught his eight children to swim in the wake of the last steamboats, where I first killed a deer with a 20-gauge crack-barrel shotgun, where my grandson landed his first thrashing catfish on a too-limber pole. Still, I often yearn for adventures on those streams with names like Seedskadee, Medicine Lodge, Sweetwater, Green, and Salmon. With hard substrates, they are resistant to meanderings and have decisive currents, whereas a bayou's turbid flow is often barely perceptible in smooth-shouldered channels that loop and swirl in a leisurely journey to the Gulf. Paddling both, I have learned, is good metaphor and better medicine for a balanced life.

That a female indigo bunting freshly arrived from Central America struck the window beside my desk and didn't survive bothers me now much more than it once would have. I live in the woods purposefully and choose to have big windows purposefully to quench my thirst for trees when I can't be outside. Having tried all the rational suggestions to prevent bird strikes, I still kill a few, maybe three or four a year. Most of the mortality occurs during spring migration, and I am not selective as to species that I dispatch—ruby-throated hummingbird, wood thrush, red-eyed vireo, red-breasted nuthatch, worm-eating warbler.

In my head I justify these deaths by the fact that I have registered the large tract of property where I live as a "Natural Area" with Louisiana Department of Wildlife & Fisheries. It's a volunteer program of citizen-based conservation in which landowners agree to protect an area and its natural elements to the best of their abilities. A very old and diverse upland hardwood/pine forest blankets part of our property, a kind of habitat now scarce in these parts as millions of acres have succumbed to pine plantations. This uncommon forest is the type of quality habitat needed by various songbirds for nesting, wintering, or migration stopovers. I am purposefully inviting them here.

In the field of wildlife management, we tend to manage populations of animals instead of individuals within the population. For instance, regarding deer, we try to maintain a healthy herd in balance with the habitat. It's more practical than focusing on specific animals. The same is true for songbirds: provide the preferred habitat and don't worry about the occasional baby bird that falls from the nest. On a landscape scale this has proven to be an effective approach, indeed the only possible tactic in many instances.

For ten thousand nights I have slept in this place on the edge of the swamp, as wild geese flew south and wild geese flew north, wings rustling the pages of my calendar, and now that I have surpassed seven decades of a life that has also included many migrations, individuals of all species seem more important. Maybe it's a softening of my hard science outlook, or perhaps it is because I've had a couple of near window strikes myself that I made the effort to bury the indigo bunting beneath my favorite wild azalea. Purposefully.

EPILOGUE

... the likes of these words being always in the back of my mind while exploring the paths of this place.

A human being is a part of the whole, called by us "Universe," a part limited in time and space. He experiences himself, his thoughts and feelings as something separated from the rest—a kind of optical delusion of his consciousness. . . . Our task must be to free ourselves from this prison by widening our circle of compassion to embrace all living creatures and the whole of nature in its beauty.

—ALBERT EINSTEIN, 1950

{ THE END }

SELECTED
BIBLIOGRAPHY

Arkansaswater.org. "Bayou D'Arbonne Watershed." May 9, 2021. https://www.ar-kansaswater.org/29-watershed/117-bayou-darbonne-8040206.

Barron, G. 2016. "Steamboats Made History in Parish." May 6, 2021. https://shilohto-canaan.com/2016/09/01/steamboats-made-history-in-parish/.

Cole, C. "Union Parish." 1892. *The Picayune,* November 6.

Curtice, K. B. 2020. *Native.* Ada, MI: Brazos Press.

Darby, W. 1816. *A Geographical Description of the State of Louisiana.* Philadelphia: John Melish.

Einstein, A. Condolence letter to Norman Salit, March 4, 1950. Reprinted in the *New York Times,* March 29, 1972.

Franks, L. O. Personal Communication, December 2, 2012.

Gates, L. "The Nature Mysticism of John Muir." Sierra Club website. May 9, 2021. https://vault.sierraclub.org/john_muir_exhibit/life/nature_mysticism_gates.aspx.

Hanks, G. Personal Communication, August 25, 2020, and other dates.

Harris, J. L. 2017. "Freshwater Mussel Survey of Overflow, Upper Ouachita, D'Arbonne, and Tensas River National Wildlife Refuges." Final Report to the US Fish and Wildlife Service.

Haskell, D. G. 2017. *The Songs of Trees: Stories from Nature's Great Connectors.* New York: Viking.

Haye, N. Personal Communication, December 8, 2013, and other dates.

Henry David Thoreau Quotes. BrainyQuote.com, BrainyMedia Inc, 2021. May 9, 2021. https://www.brainyquote.com/quotes/henry_david_thoreau_395409.

Hesse, H. 1984. *Baume*. Frankfurt: Insel.

Hranicky, W. 2009. *Material Culture from Prehistoric Virginia*. Bloomington: Authorhouse.

Hudson, T. D. 2005. "A Brief History of the European Settlement of Union Parish, Louisiana, 1540–1850." *USGenWeb Archives*. May 6, 2021. http://files.usgwarchives.net/la/union/history/history.txt.

———. 2008. "Union Parish, Louisiana Waterways." *USGenWeb Archives*. May 6, 2021. http://www.usgwarchives.net/la/union/geography/water-courses.htm.

Johnson, T. F. Unpublished diary, 1908–1909.

Kniffen, F. B., H. F. Gregory, and G. A. Stokes. 1987. *The Historic Indian Tribes of Louisiana from 1542 to Present*. Baton Rouge: Louisiana State University Press.

Kral, R. 1966. "Observations on the Flora of the Southeastern United States with Special Reference to Northern Louisiana." *SIDA* 2(6): 395–408.

Lambert, J. M. M. Personal communication, April 11, 1994.

Leopold, A. 1966. *A Sand County Almanac*. New York: Oxford University Press.

Lopez, B. H. 2019. "The World We Still Have: Barry Lopez on Restoring Our Lost Intimacy with Nature." *The Sun*, December.

Louisiana Department of Conservation. 1918. "Biennial Report, 1916–1918." New Orleans: Louisiana Dept. of Conservation.

Louisiana Department of Environmental Quality. "Fish Consumption and Swimming Advisories." May 9, 2021. https://deq.louisiana.gov/page/fishing-consumption-and-swimming-advisories.

McGuire, R. F. Diary, 1818–1852. Photocopy in Ouachita Parish Library. Monroe, LA.

McKinnie, J. 2020. "History of Rocky Branch Community." Shiloh to Canaan.com. May 9, 2021. https://shilohtocanaan.com/2020/03/30/history-of-rocky-branch-community/?fbclid=IwAR2wF-ZVHlsDuo4mUMTg9dUilj9Iwp8_M9cpGnii_cd-ncHkEPvFa3NBi62k.

Moore, C. B. 1913. "Some Aboriginal Sites in Louisiana and in Arkansas: Atchafalaya River, Lake Larto, Tensas River, Bayou Macon, and Bayou D'Arbonne in Louisiana; Saline River in Arkansas." *Journal of the Academy of Natural Sciences of Philadelphia* 16:5–99.

Moore, D. C. 1984. "A Preliminary Survey of the Vascular Flora of Union Parish, Louisiana." Unpublished Master's Thesis, Northeast Louisiana University, Monroe.

Odonata Central. June 3, 2021. https://www.odonatacentral.org/.

Ouchley, A. G. 1986. "Tanner Returns to the Tensas." *Madison Journal*, March 26.

Ouchley, J. K. Unpublished field diaries and journals, 1978–2021.

———. 2010. *Flora and Fauna of the Civil War: An Environmental Reference Guide*. Baton Rouge: Louisiana State University Press.

———. 2011. *Bayou-Diversity: Nature and People in the Louisiana Bayou Country*. Baton Rouge: Louisiana State University Press.

———. 2013. *American Alligator: Ancient Predator in the Modern World.* Gainesville: University Press of Florida.

———. 2018. *Bayou-Diversity 2: Nature and People in the Louisiana Bayou Country.* Baton Rouge: Louisiana State University Press.

———. "Don Juan Filhiol." 64 Parishes.org. May 9, 2021. https://64parishes.org/entry/don-juan-filhiol.

———. "Fort Miro." 64 Parishes.org. May 9, 2021. https://64parishes.org/entry/fort-miro.

Rees, M. A., ed. 2010. *Archaeology of Louisiana.* Baton Rouge: Louisiana State University Press.

Saunders, J. W., R. D. Mandel, R. T. Saucier, et al. 1997. "A Mound Complex in Louisiana at 5400–5000 Years before the Present." *Science* 277(5333): 1796–1799.

Schafer, H. 1952. "The Louisiana Garfish." *Louisiana Conservationist,* October.

Shorris, E. 2000. "The Last Word." *Harper's Magazine,* August.

Spillers, R. C. 2010. *Light to a Dark Corner: A History of Spencer, Louisiana.* Batesville, AR: Open Ear Publishers.

Steinberg. M. K. 2008. *Stalking the Ghost Bird: The Elusive Ivory-Billed Woodpecker in Louisiana.* Baton Rouge: Louisiana State University Press.

Tanner, J. T. 1942. *The Ivory-billed Woodpecker. National Audubon Society Research Report 1.* New York: National Audubon Society.

Union Parish, Louisiana. Police Jury Minutes, June 7, 1842, and June 6, 1843.

US Energy Information Administration. "Natural Gas Explained." May 9, 2021. https://www.eia.gov/energyexplained/natural-gas/.

US Fish and Wildlife Service. "D'Arbonne National Wildlife Refuge Annual Narrative Reports 1978–2019."

———. 2006. *D'Arbonne National Wildlife Refuge—Comprehensive Conservation Plan.*

US War Department. 1884. "Survey of D'Arbonne River, Louisiana." *Annual Report of the Secretary of War, Vol. 2.* Washington, DC: US Government Printing Office.

Wainwright, C. O. Personal Communication, various dates 1967–2010.

Walker, B. T. 1961. "A Taxonomic Survey of the Fish Fauna of Bayou D'Arbonne Drainage Prior to Impoundment." M.S. Thesis, Louisiana Polytechnic Institute, Ruston.

Werner, A. G. 1821. *Werner's Nomenclature of Colours.* Edinburgh/London: Blackwood & Cadell.

Wilson, E. O. 1998. *Consilience.* New York: Alfred A. Knopf.

Wolf, B. "Louisiana Gar Fish." 1951. *Louisiana Conservationist,* May–June.

Wood, M. G. 1981. "A Taxonomic Survey of the Fishes of Bayou D'Arbonne after Impoundment." M.S. thesis, Northeast Louisiana University, Monroe.